COGAT®

GRADE 2

MATH

3 Practice Tests
Level 8

Savant Test Prep™

www.SavantPrep.com

Please leave a review for this book!

Thank you for purchasing this resource.

Please take a moment to leave a
review on the website where you purchased this.

TABLE OF CONTENTS

INTRODUCTION

COGAT® GENERAL INFORMATION

- COGAT® stands for Cognitive Abilities Test®.
- The test measures students' reasoning skills and problem-solving skills.
- It provides educators with an overall assessment of students' academic strengths and weaknesses.
- The COGAT® is commonly used as a screener for gifted and talented programs.
    - Gifted and Talented (G&T) selection sometimes requires a teacher recommendation as well.
- The test is usually administered in a group setting.
- A teacher (or other school associate) administers the test, reading the directions.
- Please check with your school/testing site regarding its testing procedures, as these may differ.

COGAT® LEVEL 8 FORMAT

- Students in second grade take the COGAT® Level 8.
- The Quantitative (Math) has 50 questions.
- The test is divided into 3 main parts, each called a "Battery." Each Battery has three question types. See the chart below.

VERBAL BATTERY	NON-VERBAL BATTERY	QUANTITATIVE BATTERY
Picture Analogies: 18 Questions	Figure Analogies: 18 Questions	Number Puzzles: 14 Questions
Picture Classification: 18 Questions	Figure Classification: 18 Questions	Number Series: 18 Questions
Sentence Completion: 18 Questions	Paper Folding: 14 Questions	Number Analogies: 18 Questions

- Often, schools administer one Battery per day, allowing approximately 45 minutes per Battery.
- Students have around 15 minutes to complete each question type (for example, students would have around 15 minutes to complete Picture Analogies).
- See the following pages for examples and explanations of each question type.

COGAT® SCORING

- Students receive points for correct answers. Points are not deducted for incorrect answers. (Therefore, students should at least guess versus leaving a question blank.)
- In general, schools have a "cut-off" COGAT® score, which they consider together with additional criteria, for gifted & talented acceptance. This varies by school.
- This score is usually at least 98%. (However, some schools accept scores of 95% or even 85%.)
- A score of 98% means that your child scored as well as, or better than, 98% of those in his/her testing group.
- COGAT® scores are available for the entire test and can be broken down by Battery.
- Depending on the school/program, such a "cut-off" score may only be required on one or two of the Batteries (and not on the test overall).
- It is essential to check with your school/program for their acceptance procedures.
- The COGAT® Practice Tests in this book can not yield these percentiles because they have not been given to a large enough group of students to produce an accurate comparison/calculation.)

HOW TO USE THIS BOOK

1. Go over the Question Examples together with your child. These begin on the next page.

2. Do Practice Test 1 (Workbook Format).
   - Do these questions with your child, especially if this is your child's first exposure to COGAT®-prep questions. These questions have a "workbook format," meaning they are meant to be done together.
   - Do not assign a time limit.
   - Talk about what the question is asking your child to do.
   - Questions progress in difficulty. (The first few questions are quite simple.)
   - Go over the answers using the Answer Key.
   - For questions missed, go over the answers again, discussing what makes the correct answer better than the other choices.

3. Do the remaining Practice Tests following Practice Test 1.
   - If your child progressed easily through Practice Test 1, see how well they can do without your help.
   - If your child needed assistance with much of Practice Test 1, then continue to assist your child with Practice Test 2.
   - If you wish to assign a time limit, assign around 15 minutes per question type.
   - Go over the answers using the Answer Key.
   - For questions missed, go over the answers again, discussing what makes the correct answer better than the other choices.

4. Need more practice?

   - **Get 300+ new questions per book.**

   - **Check out Savant Test Prep™ books on Amazon®.**

TEST-TAKING TIPS

- Ensure your child listens carefully to the directions.
- Make sure (s)he does not rush through questions. (There is no prize for finishing first!) Tell your child to look carefully at the question. Then, tell your child to look at each answer choice before marking his/her answer.
  - If you notice your child continuing to rush through the questions, tell him/her to point to each part of the question. Then, point to each answer choice.
- If (s)he does not know the answer, then use the process of elimination. Cross out any answer choices which are clearly incorrect, then choose from those remaining.
- This tip/suggestion is entirely at your discretion. You may wish to offer some sort of special motivation to encourage your child to do his/her best. An extra incentive of, for example, an art set, a building block set, or a special outing can go a long way in motivating young learners!
- The night before testing, it is imperative that children have enough sleep, without any interruptions. (Think about the difference in **your** brain function with a good night's sleep vs. without. The same goes for your child's brain function.)
- The morning before the test, ensure your child eats a healthy breakfast with protein and complex carbs. Do not let them eat sugar, chocolate, etc.
- If you can choose the time your child will take the test (for example, if (s)he will take the test individually, instead of at school with a group), opt for a morning testing session, when your child will be most alert.

QUESTION EXAMPLES

- Here is an overview of the COGAT® question types.
- This section has <u>simple</u> examples, to introduce your child to test concepts.
    - Do these examples together with your child.
- Below the questions are explanations for parents.

1. NUMBER ANALOGIES (QUANTITATIVE BATTERY)

• **Directions (read to child):** The pictures in the top boxes go together in some way. Look at the bottom boxes. One box is empty. Look at the row of answer choices next to the boxes. Which one of these choices goes with the picture in the bottom box like the pictures in the top box go together?

• **Explanation (read to child):** In the left box there are 7 objects (stars). In the right box there are 2 objects. From left to right, we see that 5 objects have been taken away. So, the rule here is "5 are taken away" or "-5." In the bottom left box there are 9 objects. If you have 9, and our rule is that "5 are taken away," that means the answer is 4. The third answer choice is correct.

•**Tip:** Some analogies involve addition and subtraction, while others require children to do more complex calculations: dividing in half, doubling, or tripling. If your child first tries to add or subtract, but no answer choice matches the "rule", then try to double or triple (if the number increases from left to right) or try to halve (if the number decreases from left to right).

• Show your child the example below.

• **Explanation (read to child):** In the top left box, there are 2 stars. In top right box, there is 1 star. Let's try the rule "take away 1." In the bottom left box, there are 4 stars. If our rule is "take away 1," then the answer should be 3 stars. However, there isn't an answer choice with 3 stars. Let's look again at the top boxes. If you divide 2 in half, you get 1. Let's try the rule "divide in half." If you take the 4 stars in the bottom left box and divide them in half, you get 2. The choice with 2 stars is correct.

2. NUMBER SERIES (QUANTITATIVE BATTERY)

• **Directions (read to child):** Which rod should go in the place of the missing rod to finish the pattern?

• **Explanation for #1 (read to child):** Before the missing rod, the other rods have made a pattern that we need to figure out. Then, we will complete the pattern with the correct answer choice. From left to right, we see that the pattern is: 1 - 2 - 1 - 2 - 1. After 1, comes 2. This means that the missing rod needs 2 beads.

• Make sure your child accurately counts the number of beads. In the examples below, there are numbers under the rods indicating the number of beads. The practice test questions do not have these numbers.

• After you do #1, go over questions #2 - #7 together. The pattern and the answer are already given.

1.

Pattern: the number of beads decreases by 1. The answer is 1.

2.

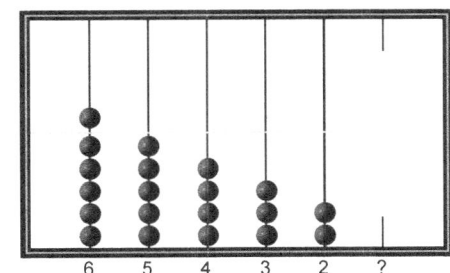  

Pattern: every other rod increases by 1. And, the alternate rods equal 0. The answer is 0.

3.

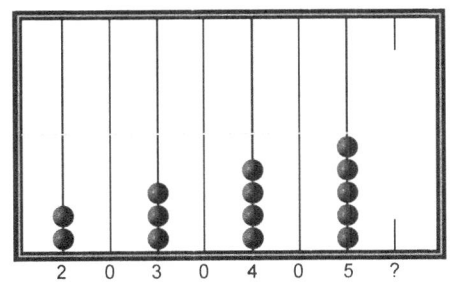   

Pattern: the rods repeat 7 - 5 - 3. The answer is 7.

4.

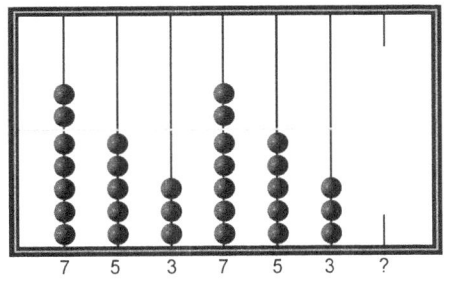  

This one may be challenging. Every other rod increases by one (1 - 2 - 3 - 4). Then, every other rod (the alternate rods), increases by one (4 - 5 - 6 - 7). With the alternating rods increasing 1, 2, 3, 4, this means that the next rod will be 5.

5.

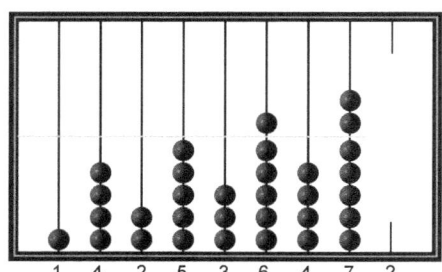  

This one may be challenging also. Every other rod decreases by one (5 - 4 - 3). Then, every other rod (the alternate rods), increases by one (1 - 2 - 3). With the alternating rods decreasing 5, 4, 3 this means that the next rod will be 2.

6.

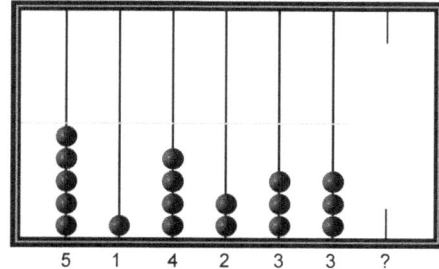

Pattern: the rods decrease with the pattern 6 - 4 - 2, then increase with the reverse pattern 2 - 4 - 6.

7.

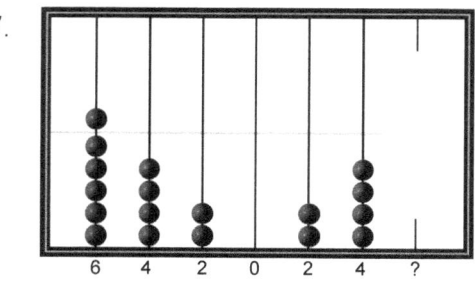  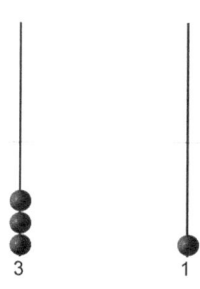

3. NUMBER PUZZLES (QUANTITATIVE BATTERY)

- **Directions (read to child):** Which number would be in place of the question mark so that both of the sides of this equal sign are the same?

- **Explanation:** This section is straightforward. Make sure your child pays attention to the plus and minus signs.

4	=	11	+	3	-	?

9   10   11   4

Ten is the answer.

Parents, read the below with your child.

Watch out!

This book is filled with tricky questions. Can you answer them?

 Of course you can!

Pay close attention to each question and try your best.

We'll be here to help you along the way!

Practice Test 1 (Workbook Format) begins on the next page.

COGAT® PRACTICE TEST 1
(WORKBOOK FORMAT)

NUMBER ANALOGIES

Sara

What goes in the empty box?

Explanation (for parents): A more detailed explanation of Number Analogies is on p.6. Look over p.6, if you have not already. Your child must figure out how the images in the top set of boxes are related mathematically. Then, (s)he must figure out which answer choice would go with the bottom left image so that the bottom set would have the same relationship. After counting the objects in the boxes, you may want your child to write the number by the box, so (s)he does not forget the quantity.

Directions for the example: Look at the top box on the left. There are 10 circles. Look at the top box on the right. There are 2 circles. What has changed from the picture on the left to the picture on the right? We need to come up with a "rule" to describe what has happened. The right box will have 8 less than the left box.

Next, let's look carefully at the bottom row. What do you see in the left box? There are 9 circles. Look at the right box. It is empty.

Look carefully at the row of pictures next to the boxes. These are the answer choices Which one of these goes in the empty box? Remember, our rule is that the right box will have 8 less than the left box. If the left box has 9 circles, and our rule is that the right box will have 8 less, then that means 1 circle is the answer. Choice B has 1 circle.

Directions for the rest: Which answer choice would go inside the empty box at the bottom?

1.

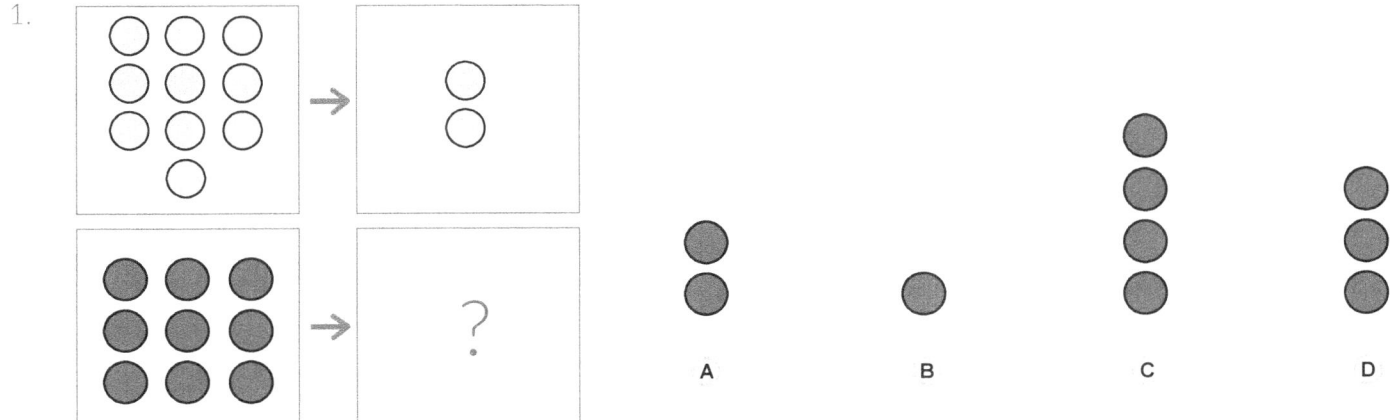

A   B   C   D

2.

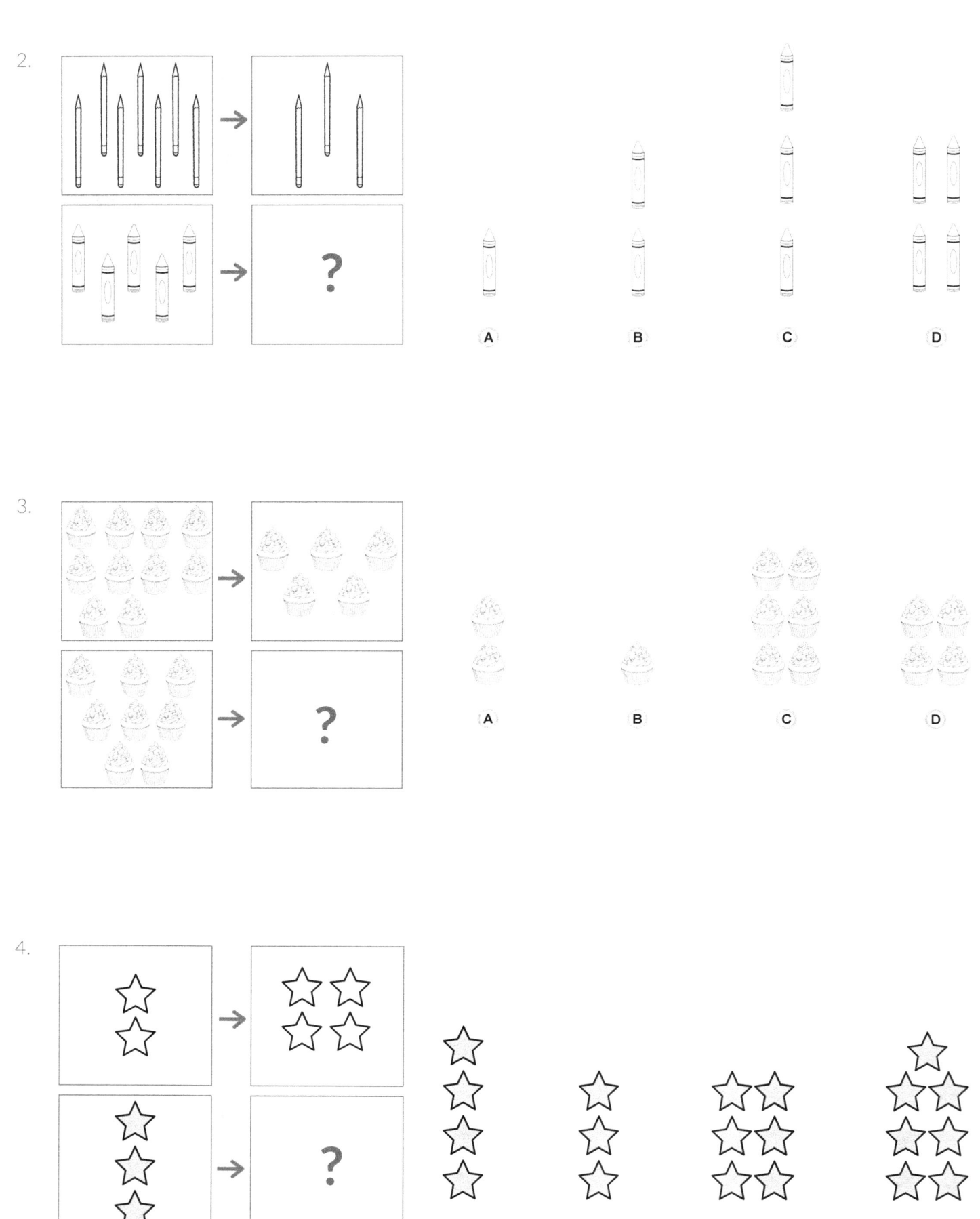

3.

4.

5.

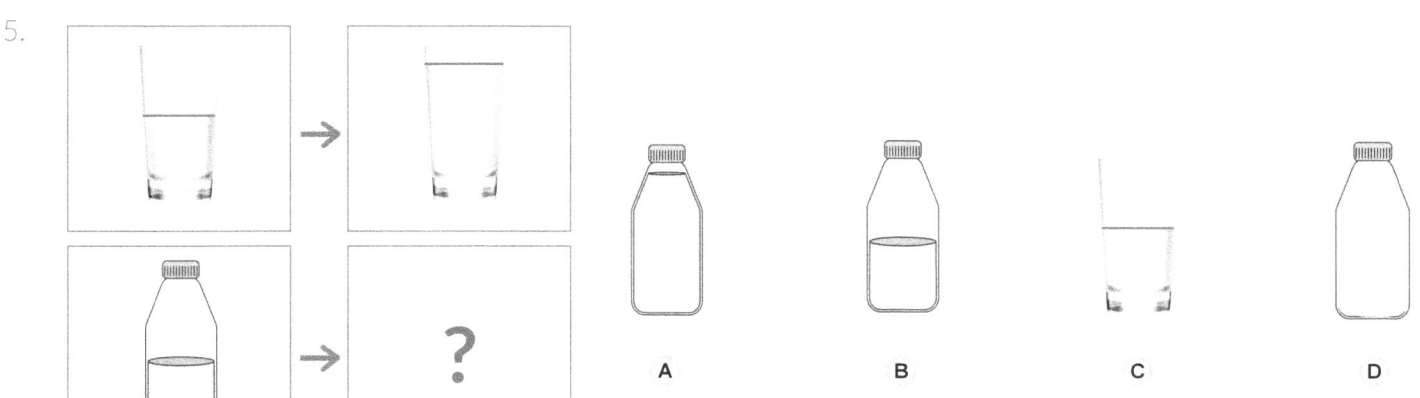

A   B   C   D

6.

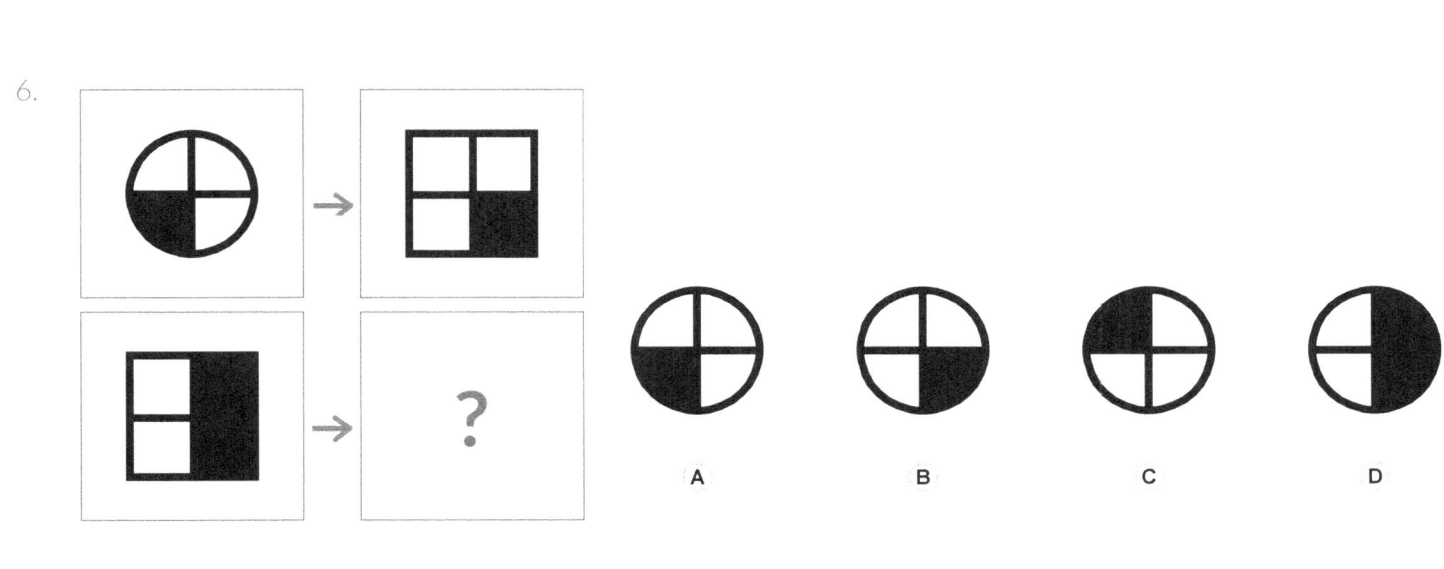

A   B   C   D

7.

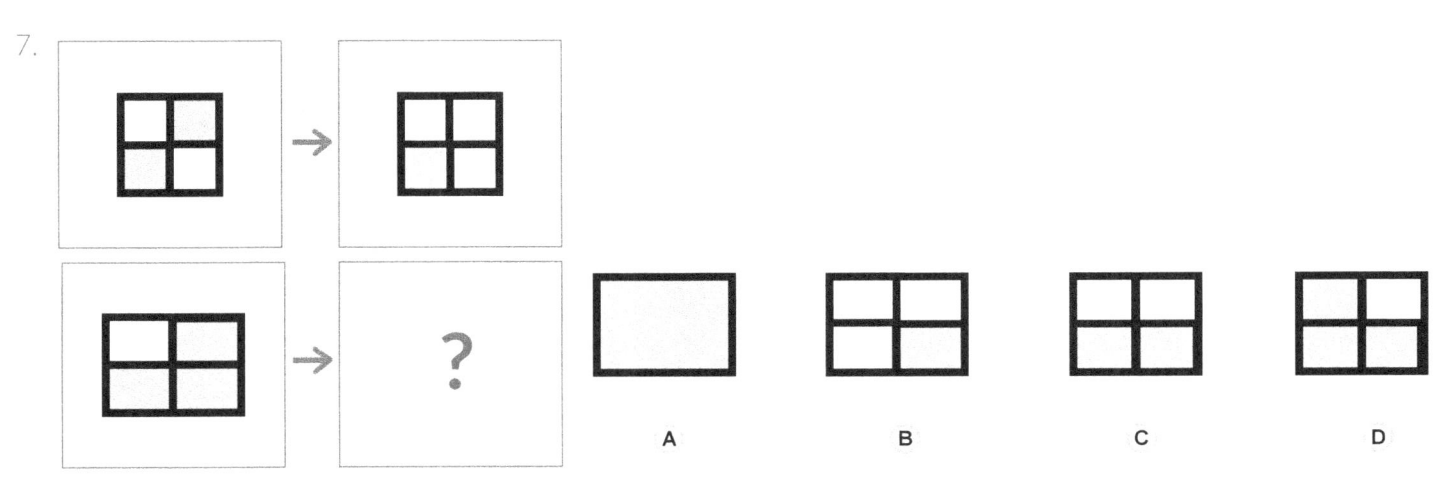

A   B   C   D

8.

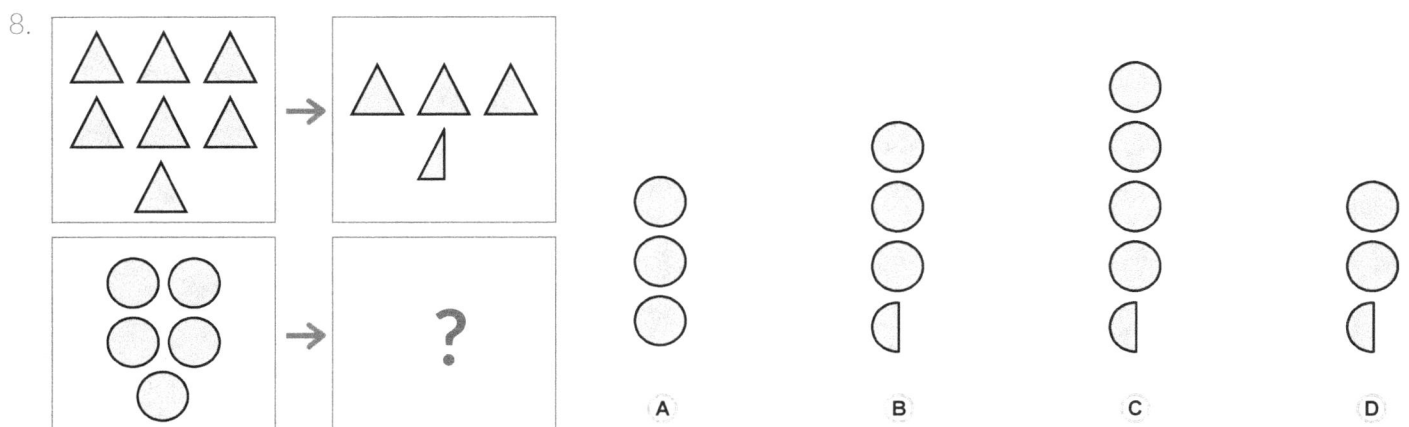

9.

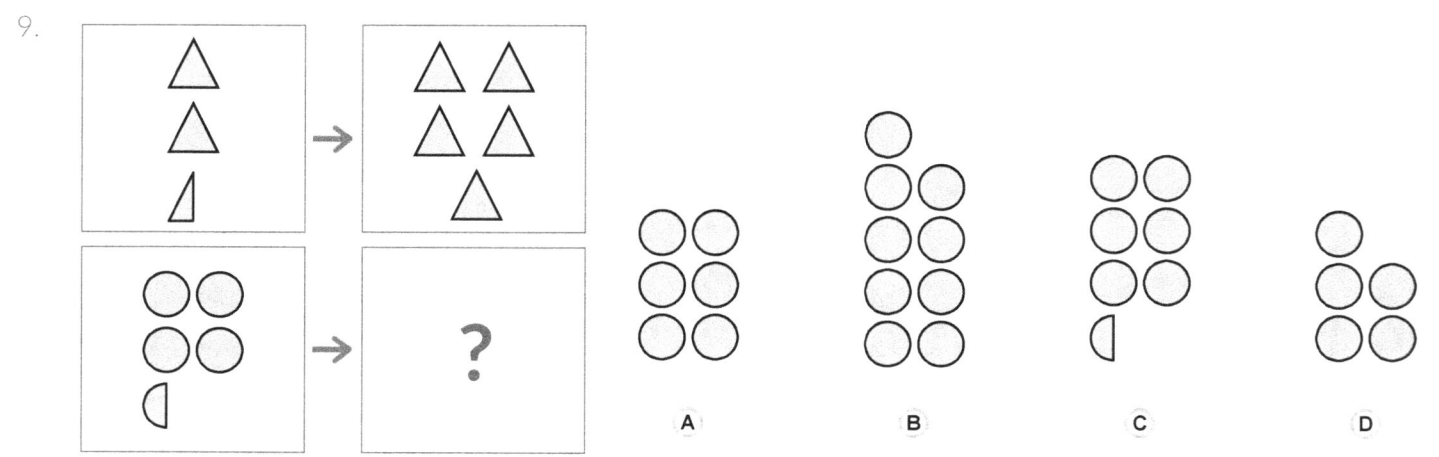

10.

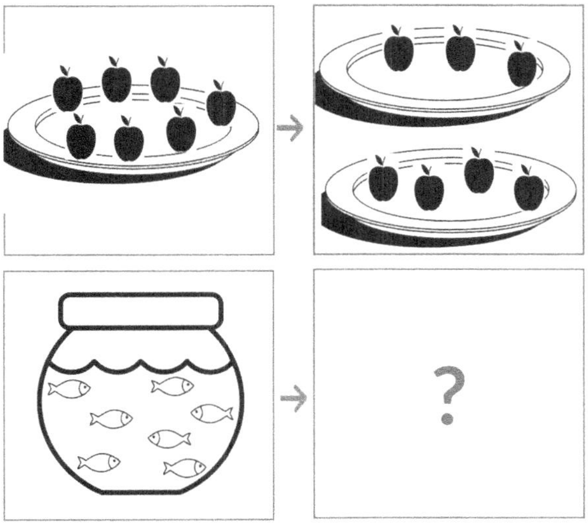

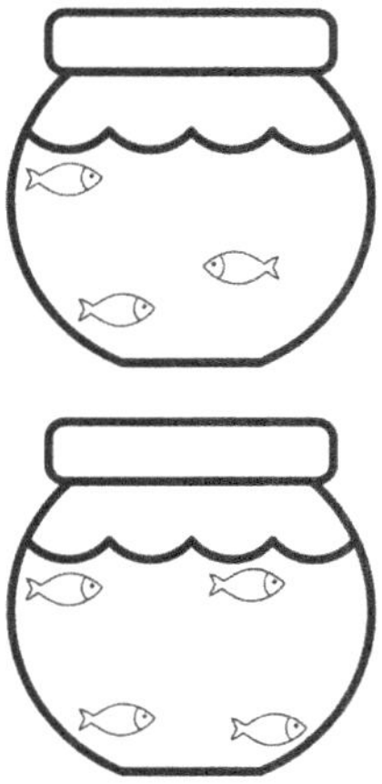

A

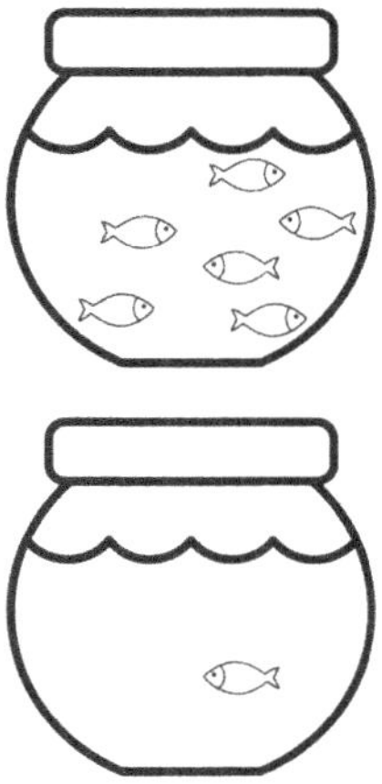

B

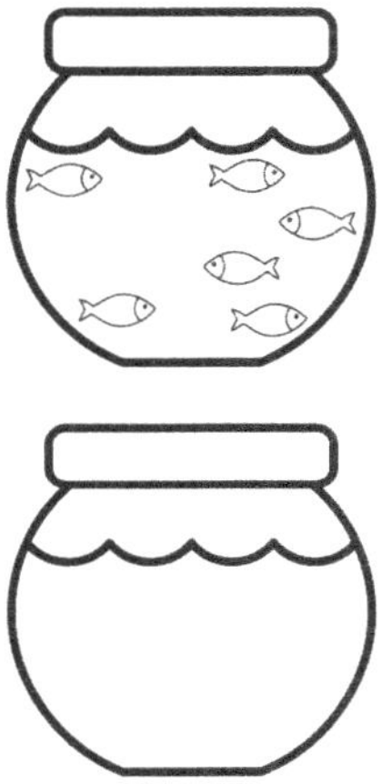

C

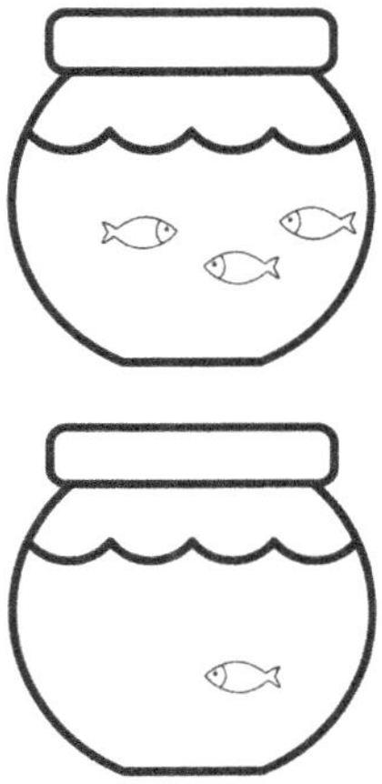

D

11.

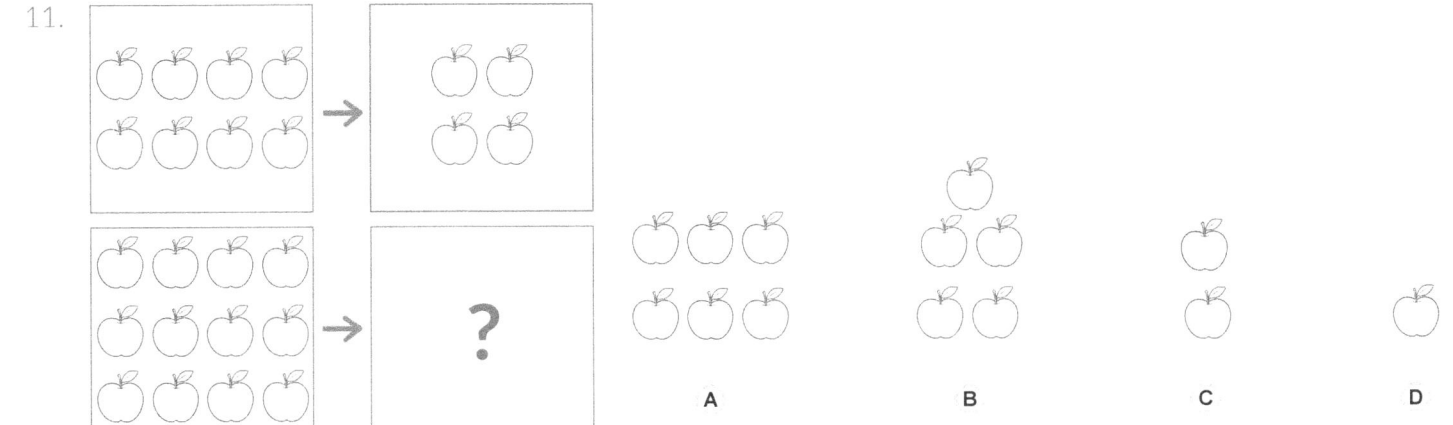

A   B   C   D

12.

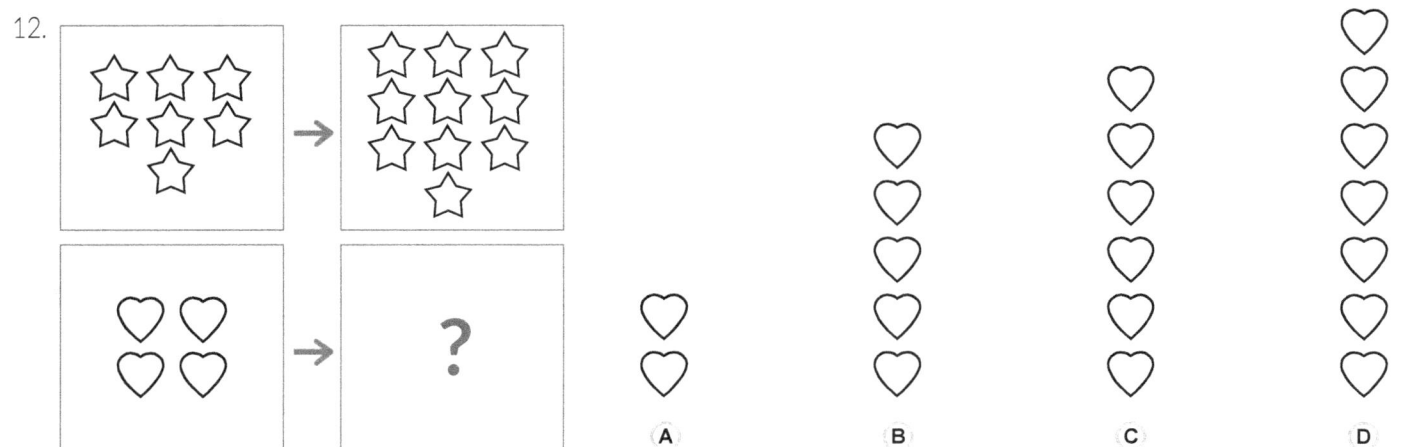

A B C D

13.

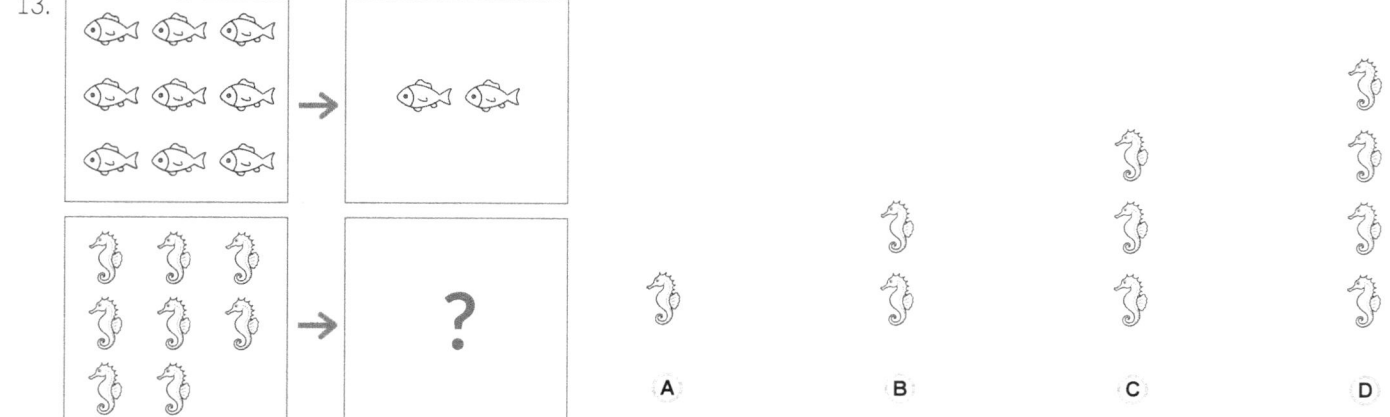

A B C D

16

14.

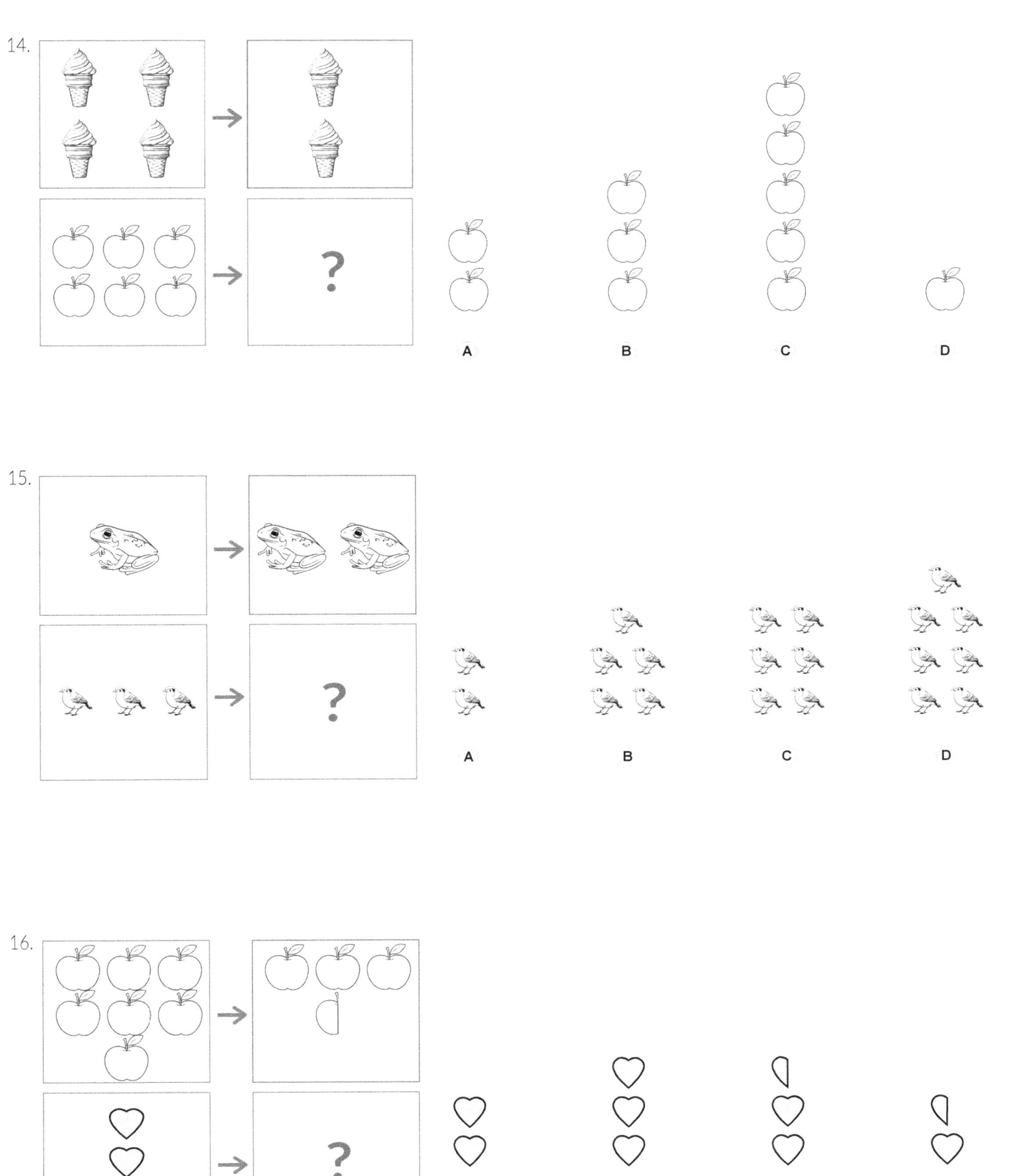

15.

16.

A   B   C   D

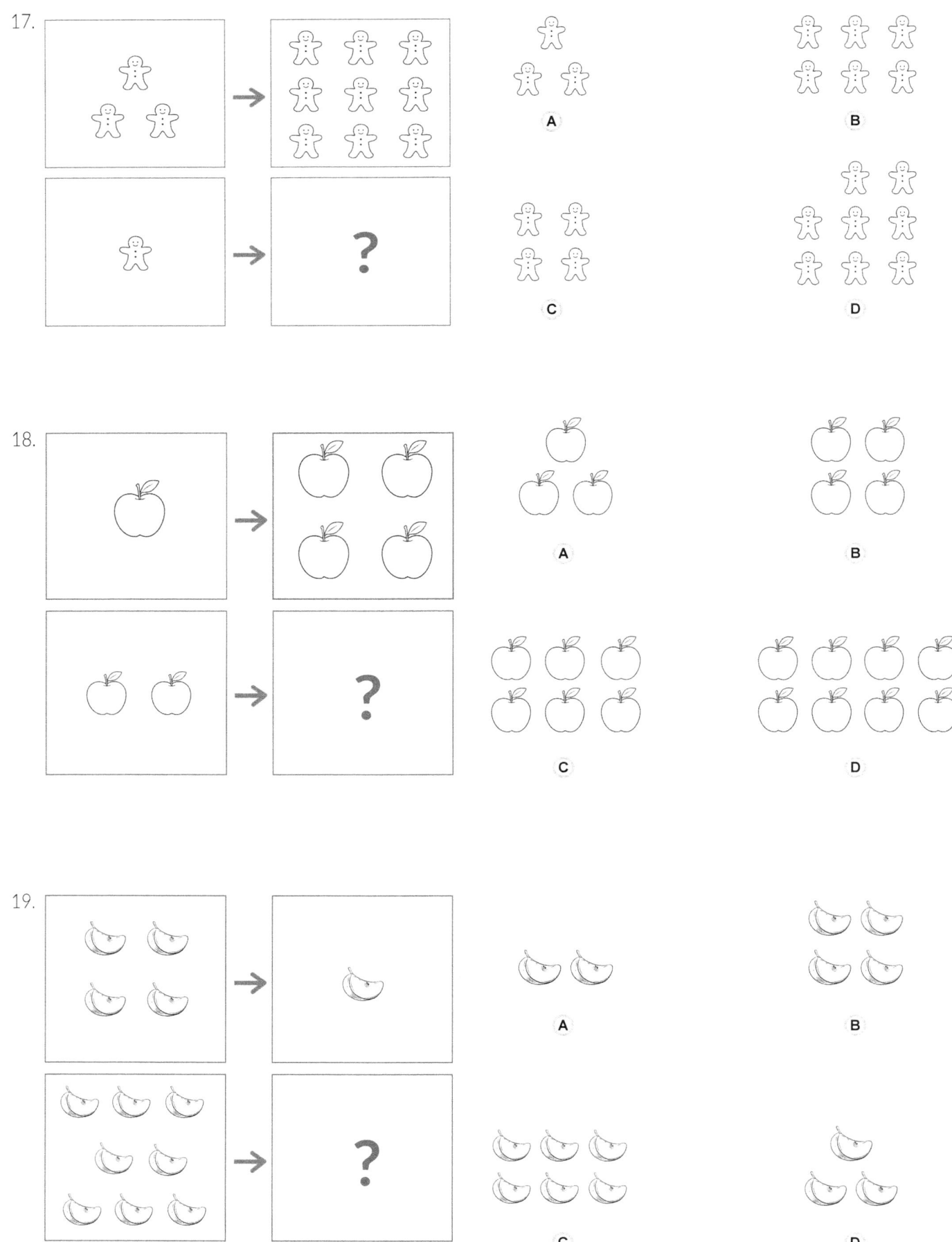

17.

A

B

C

D

18.

A

B

C

D

19.

A

B

C

D

NUMBER PUZZLES

Which number should you pick?

Kai

Directions: Look at the box that has the question mark. Which number would go here so that both of the sides of this equal sign (point to the equal sign) would have the same amount?

Parent Note: Some exercises require three numbers to be added/subtracted. In these, be sure your child correctly distinguishes between the addition and subtraction signs and completes the entire exercise before selecting an answer.

1.

9 = 4 + ?

4	5	6	7
A	B	C	D

2.

7 = 10 - ?

7	5	3	1
A	B	C	D

3.

2 = 10 - 4 - ?

1	2	3	4
A	B	C	D

4.

$12 = 6 + 6 + \boxed{?}$

0	1	2	3
A	B	C	D

5.

$11 = 9 + 5 - \boxed{?}$

4	3	2	1
A	B	C	D

6.

$2 = 12 + 0 - \boxed{?}$

8	9	10	11
A	B	C	D

7.

$5 = 3 + 11 - \boxed{?}$

10	9	8	7
A	B	C	D

8.

$10 = 0 + 12 - \boxed{?}$

5	4	3	2
A	B	C	D

9.

$7 = 12 - 3 - \boxed{?}$

2	1	0	3
A	B	C	D

10.

$12 = 11 - 9 + \boxed{?}$

9
A

12
B

11
C

10
D

11.

$11 = 15 - 8 + \boxed{?}$

3
A

4
B

5
C

6
D

12.

$2 = 15 - 9 - \boxed{?}$

6
A

5
B

4
C

3
D

13.

$0 = 14 - 7 - \boxed{?}$

7
A

6
B

5
C

4
D

14.

$15 = 8 + 3 + \boxed{?}$

10
A

4
B

5
C

6
D

15.

$13 = 2 + 1 + \boxed{?}$

11
A

12
B

9
C

10
D

NUMBER SERIES

Let's figure out the pattern!

Maya

Directions (read to child): Which rod should go in the place of the missing rod to finish the pattern?

Explanation (for parents): The final rod of the abacus is missing. Before this missing rod, the rods of the abacus have made a pattern. Your child must look closely to determine the pattern.

Go over p.7 with your child, if you haven't already.

Note that some rods do not have any beads. Rods without any beads equal "0." The gray line appears above the 5th bead's place.

Example (read to child): The picture below shows an abacus. The abacus has rods going from the bottom to the top. On these rods are beads. These rods have made a pattern that we need to figure out.

First, we see a rod with 7 beads. Then, we see 6 beads, 5 beads, 4 beads, and 3 beads. Then, finally there is a missing rod. What is the pattern that these rods have made? Each time, there is one less bead. If this is the pattern, what should the next rod be after 3 (the rod that would go in place of the missing rod on the abacus)?

The rod with 2 beads, choice A.

1.

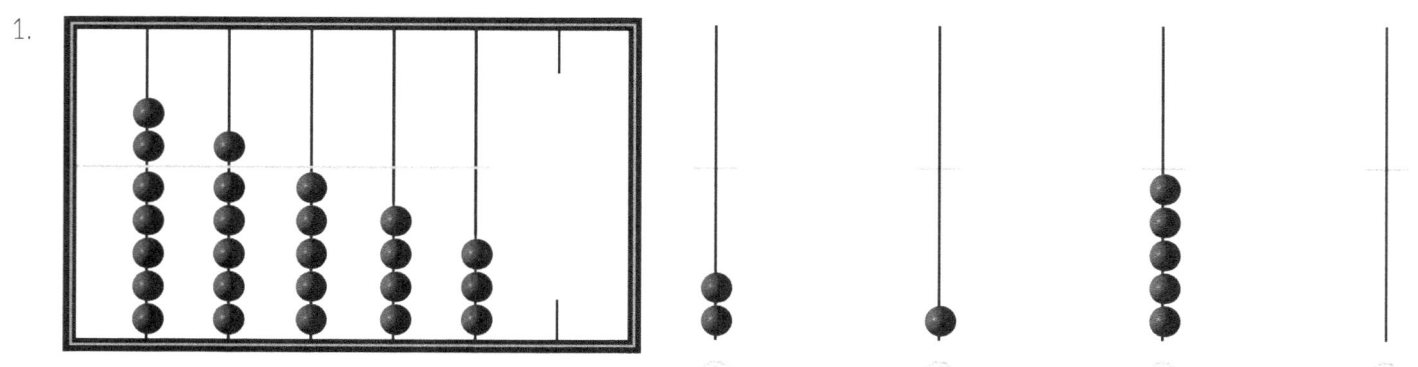

2.

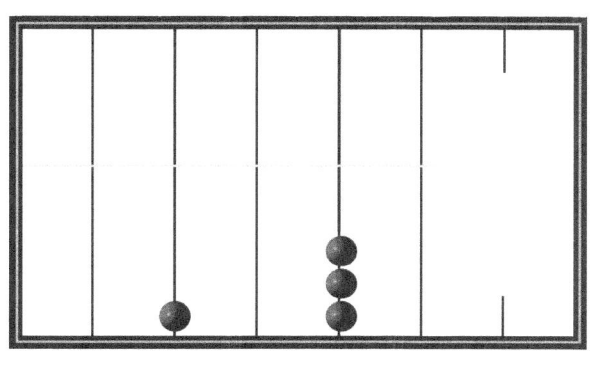

A   B   C   D

3.

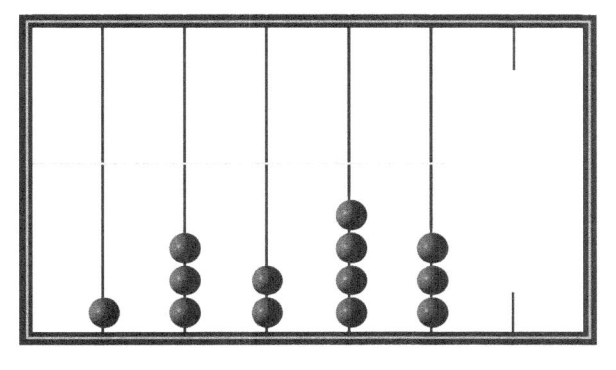

A   B   C   D

4.

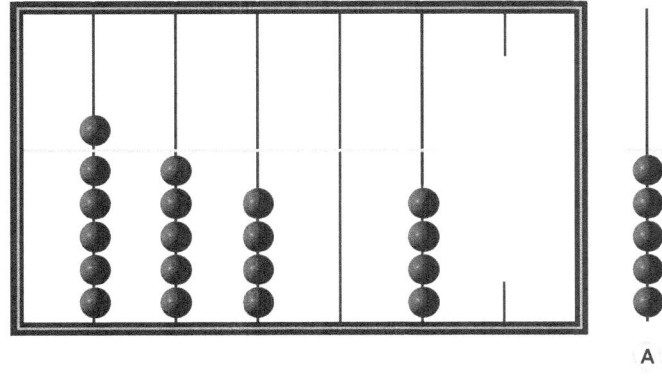

A   B   C   D

5.

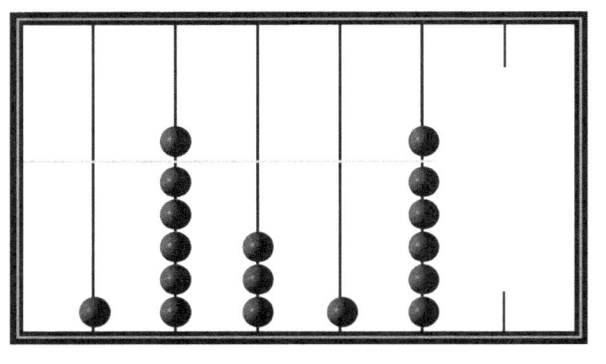

A   B   C   D

6.

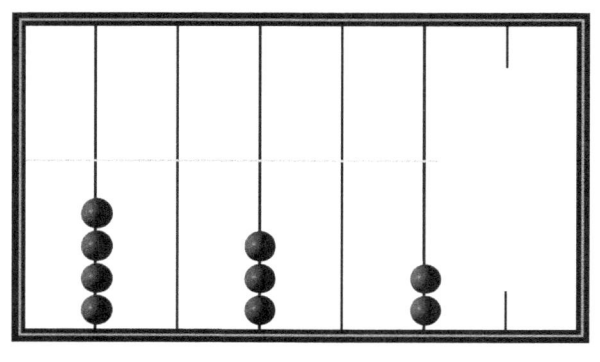

A   B   C   D

7.

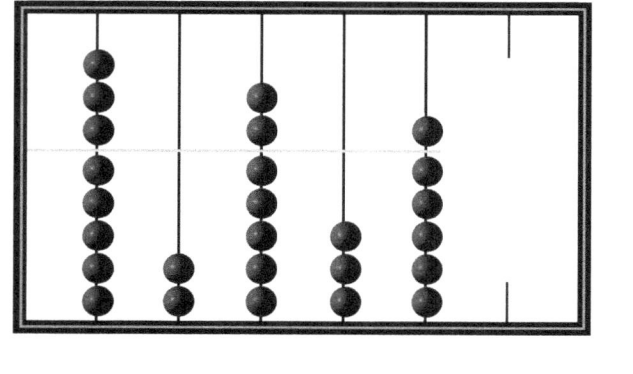

A   B   C   D

24

8.

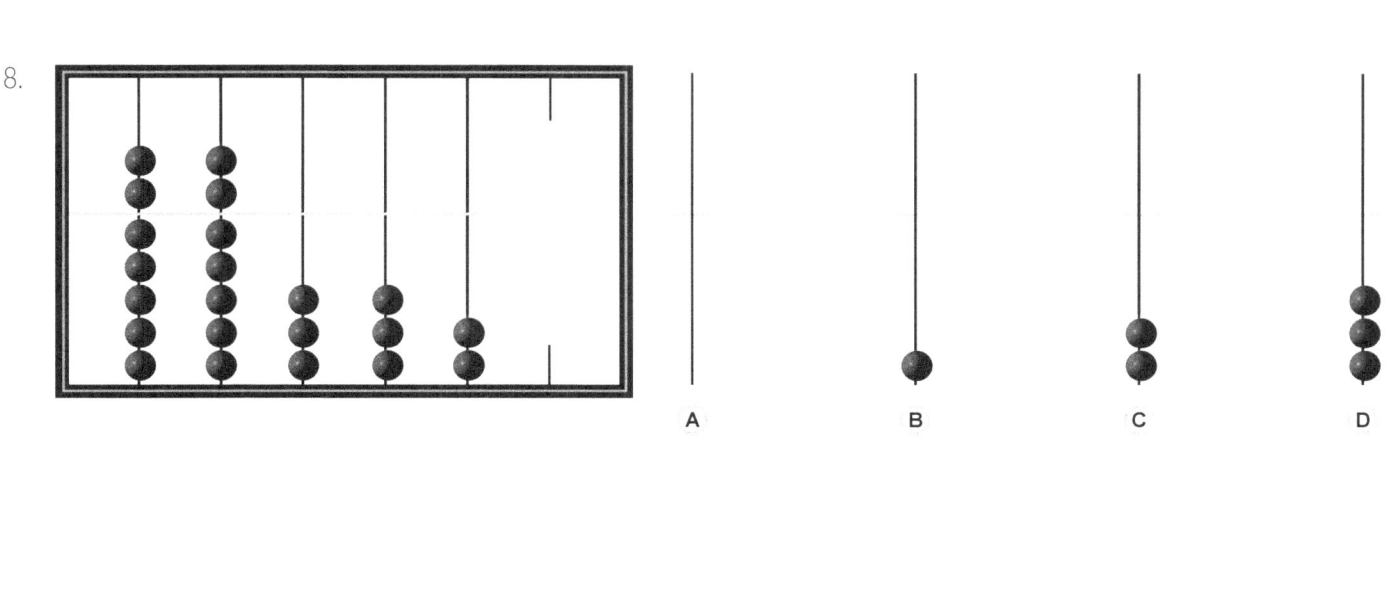

A   B   C   D

9.

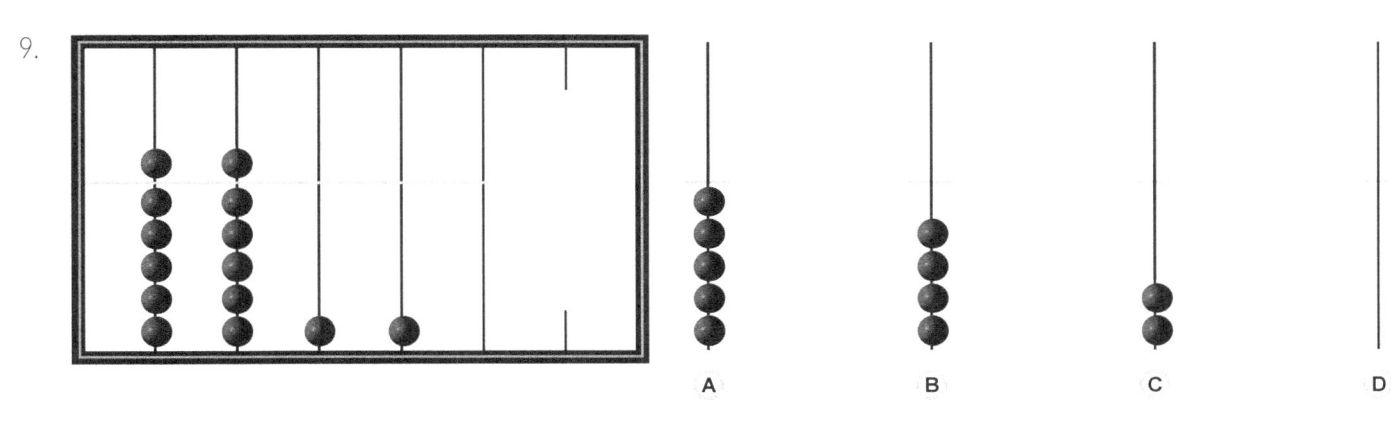

A   B   C   D

10.

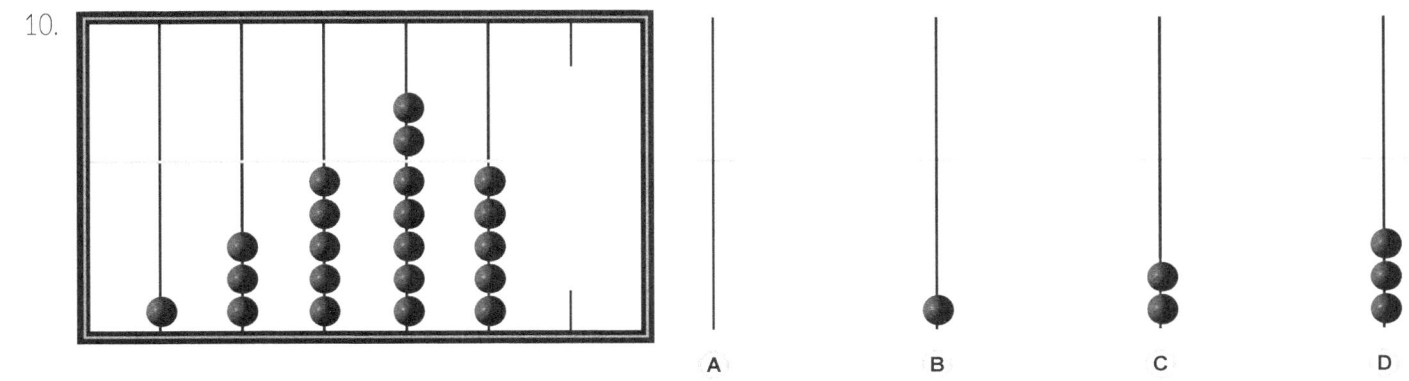

A   B   C   D

11.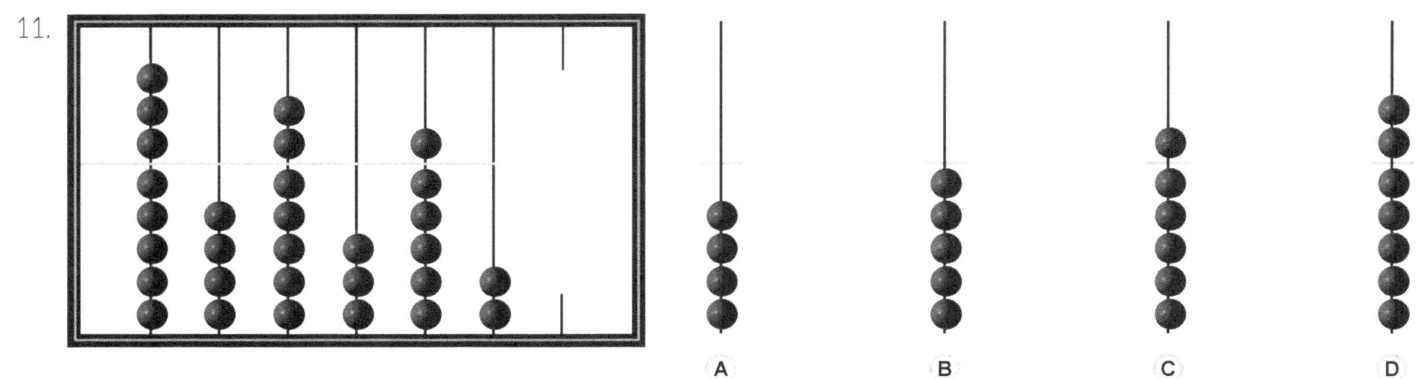

A   B   C   D

12.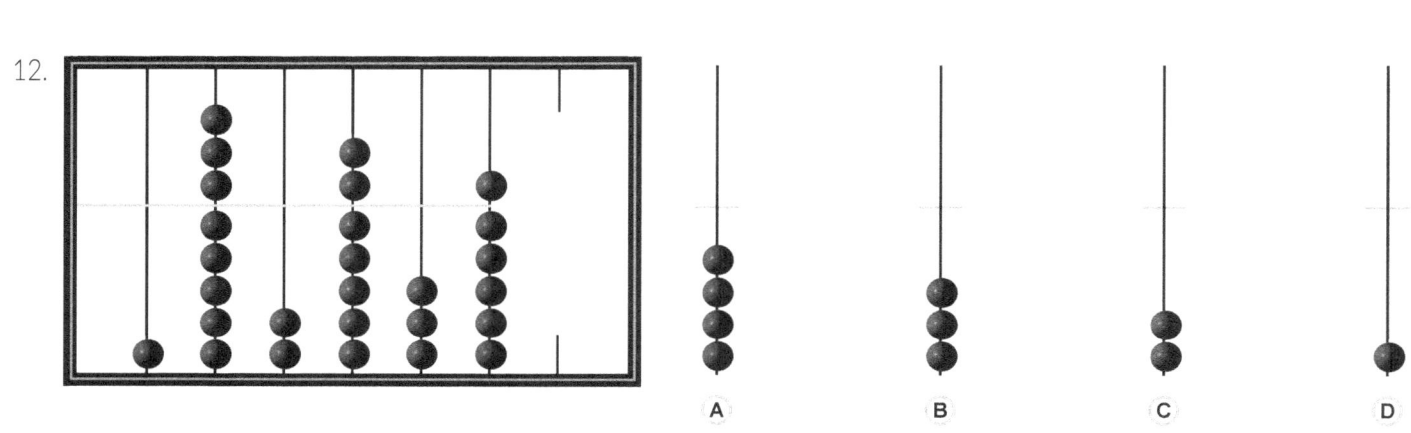

A   B   C   D

13.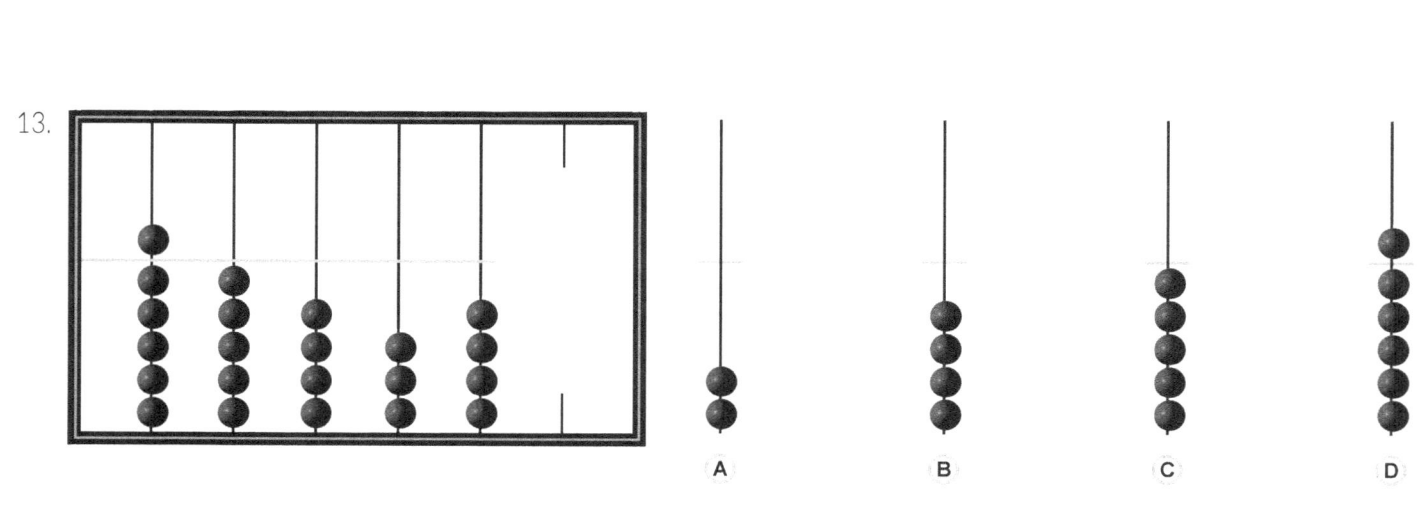

A   B   C   D

26

14.

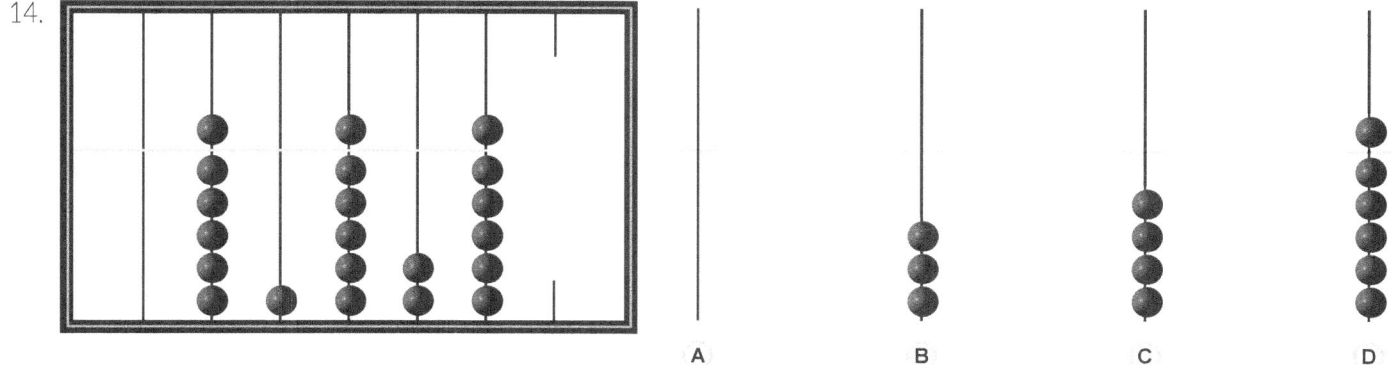

A   B   C   D

15.

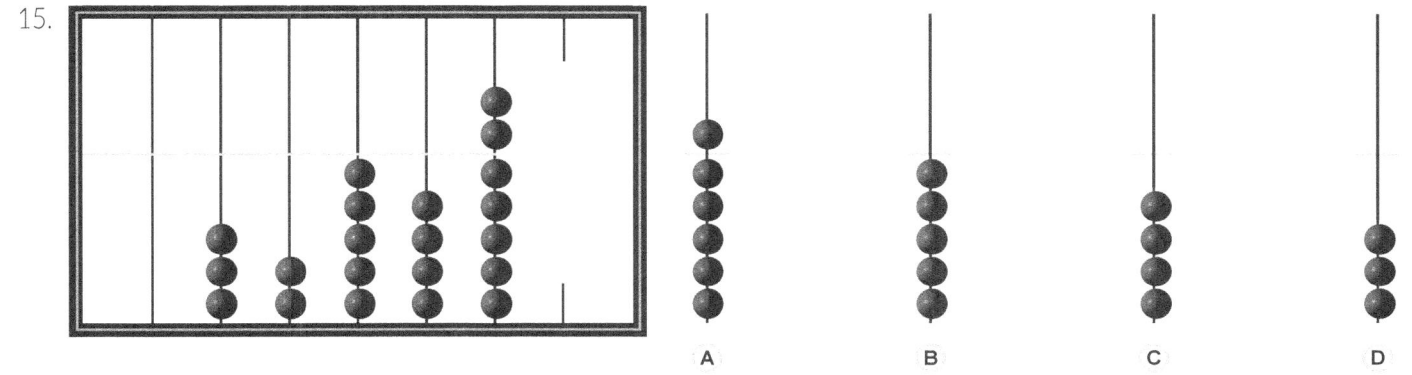

A   B   C   D

16.

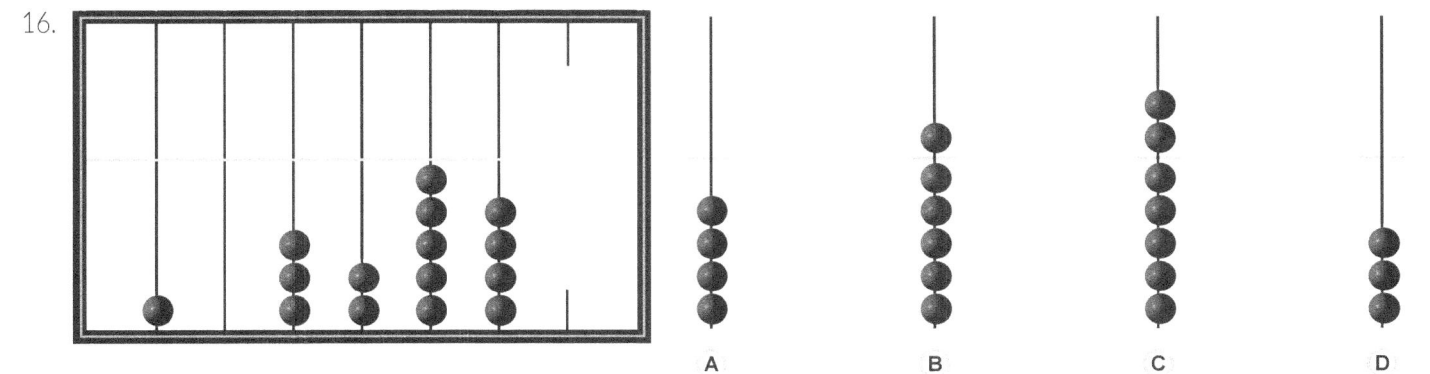

A   B   C   D

17.

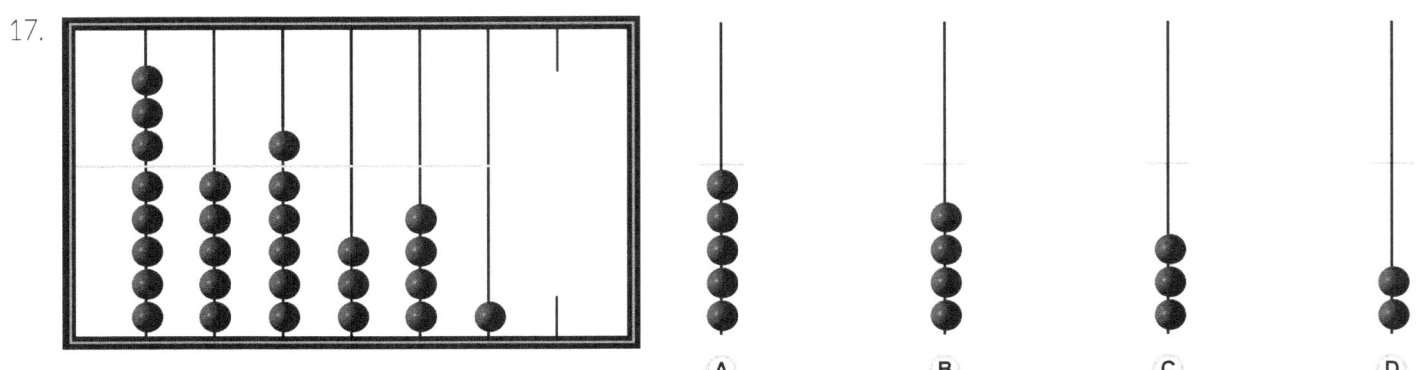

18.

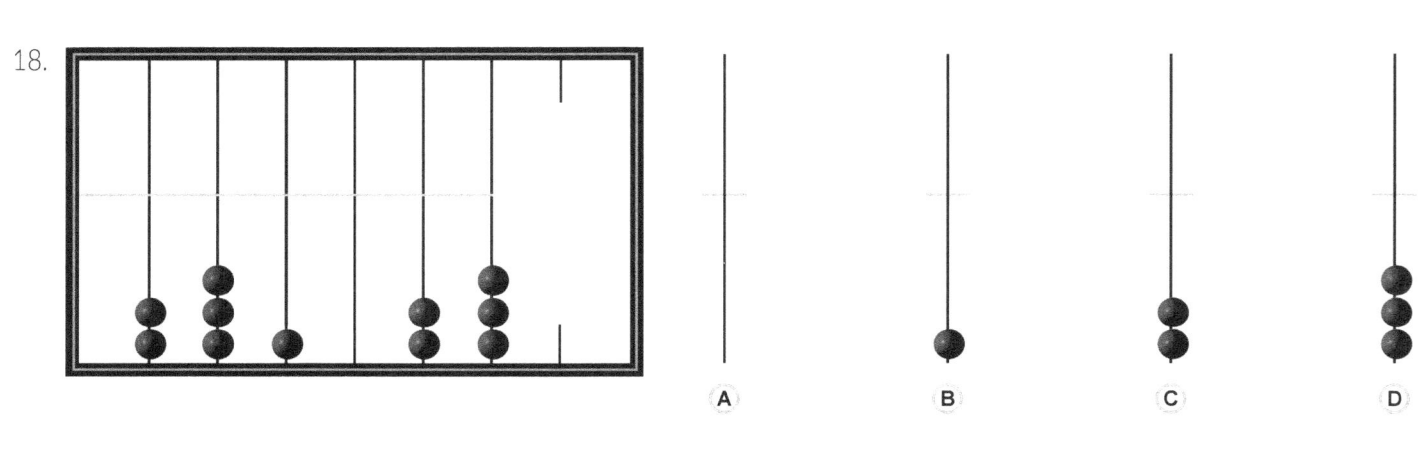

Keep up the good work!

Noah

- End of Practice Test 1 (Workbook Format) -

COGAT® PRACTICE TEST 2

Which answer choice goes with the picture in the bottom box in the same way the top pictures do?

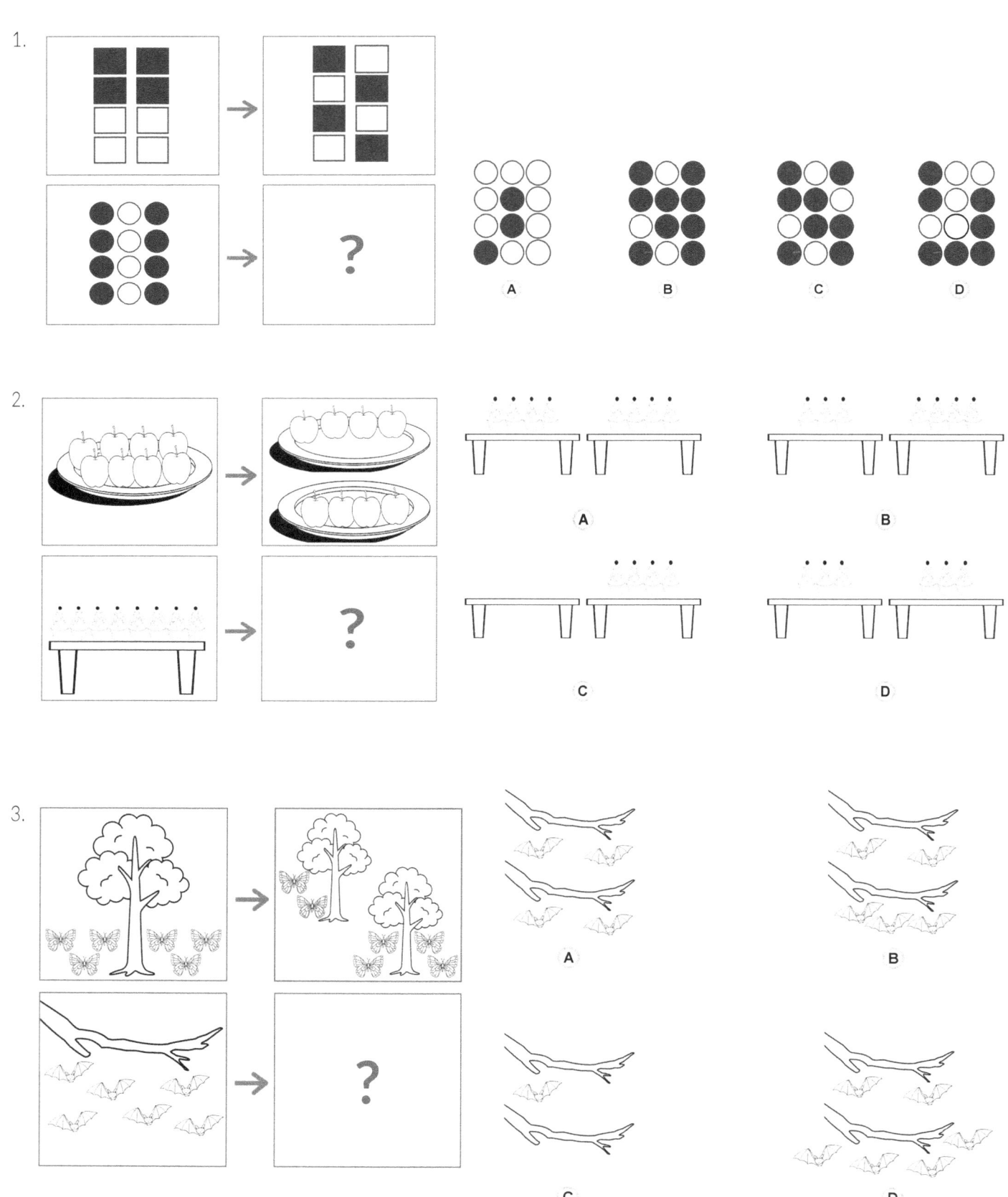

4.

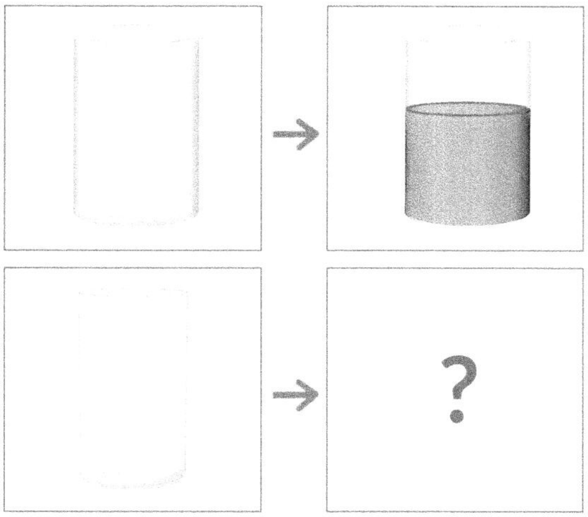

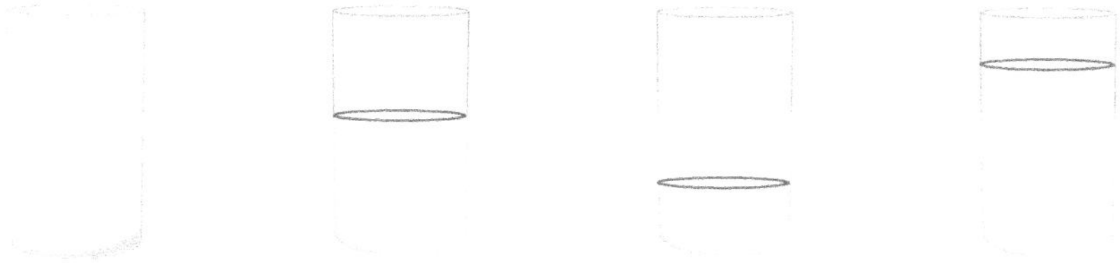

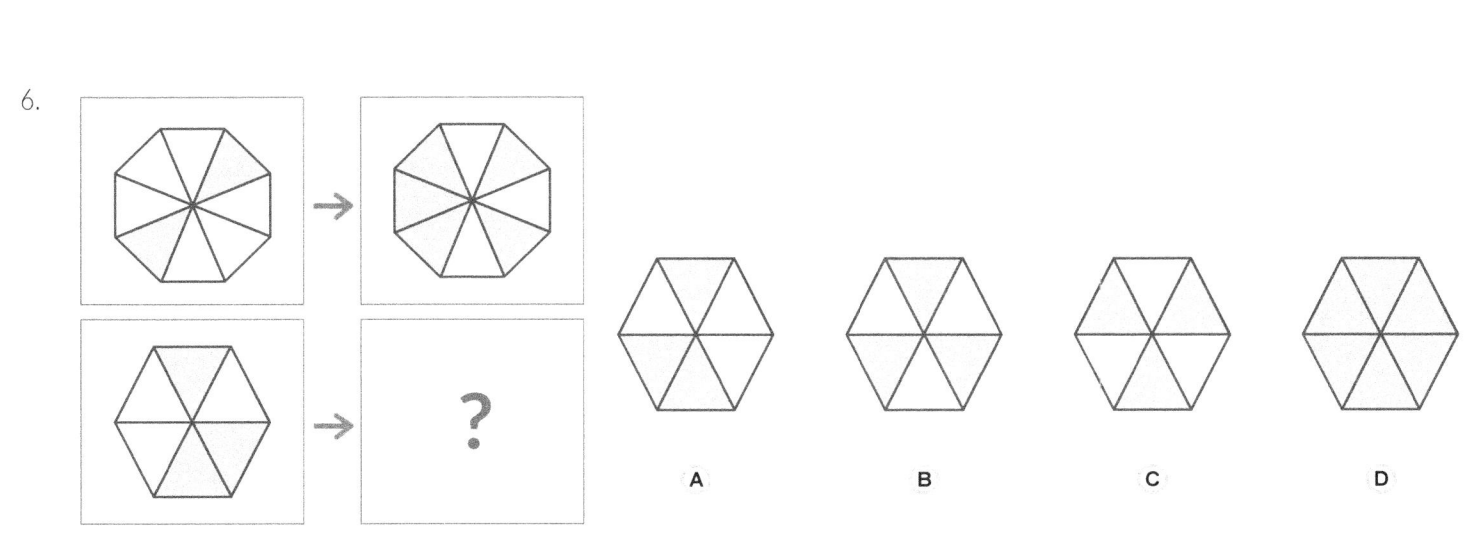

5.

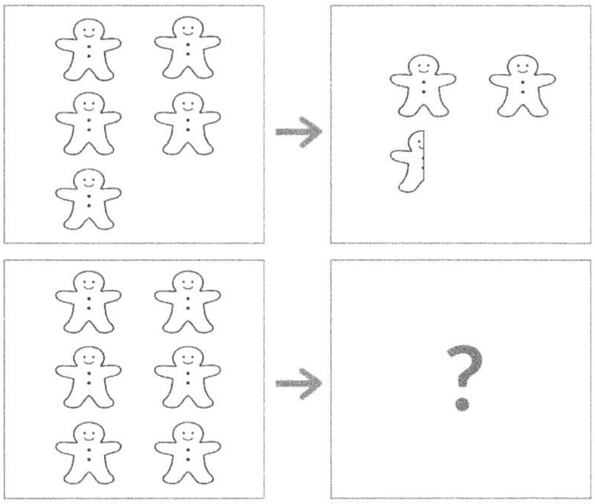

6.

7.

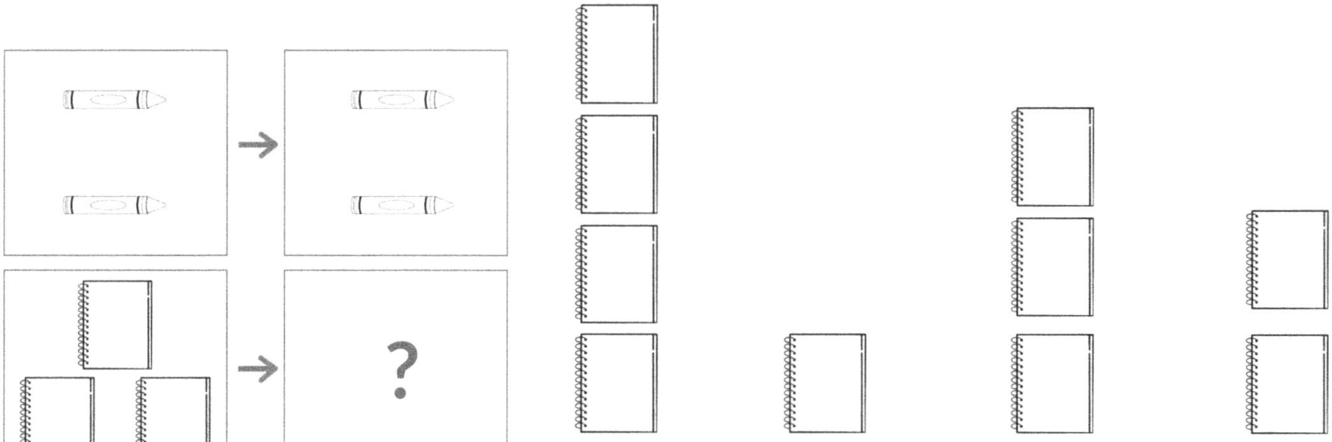

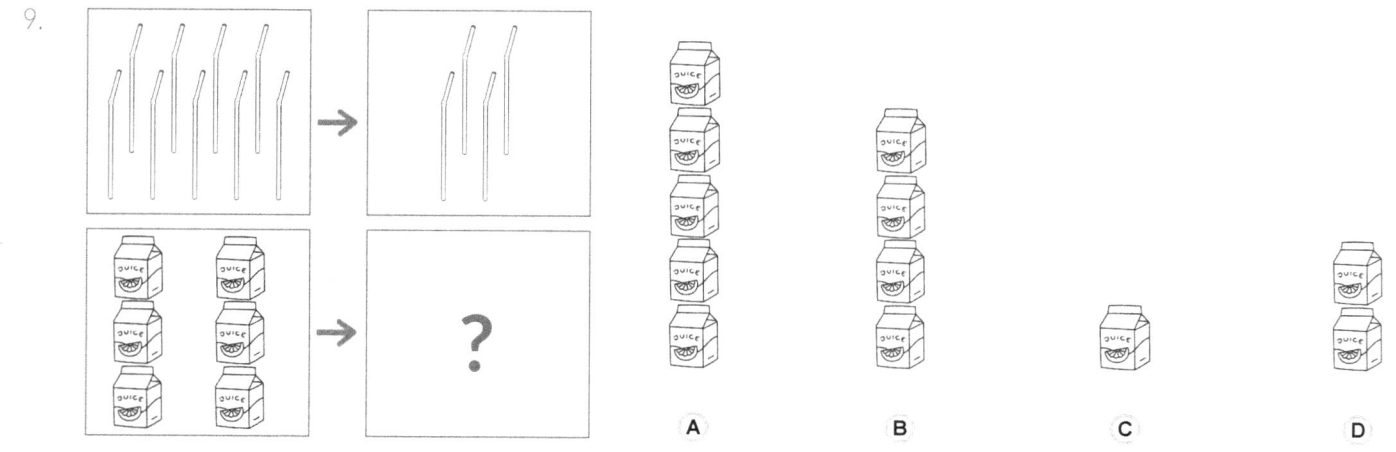

8.

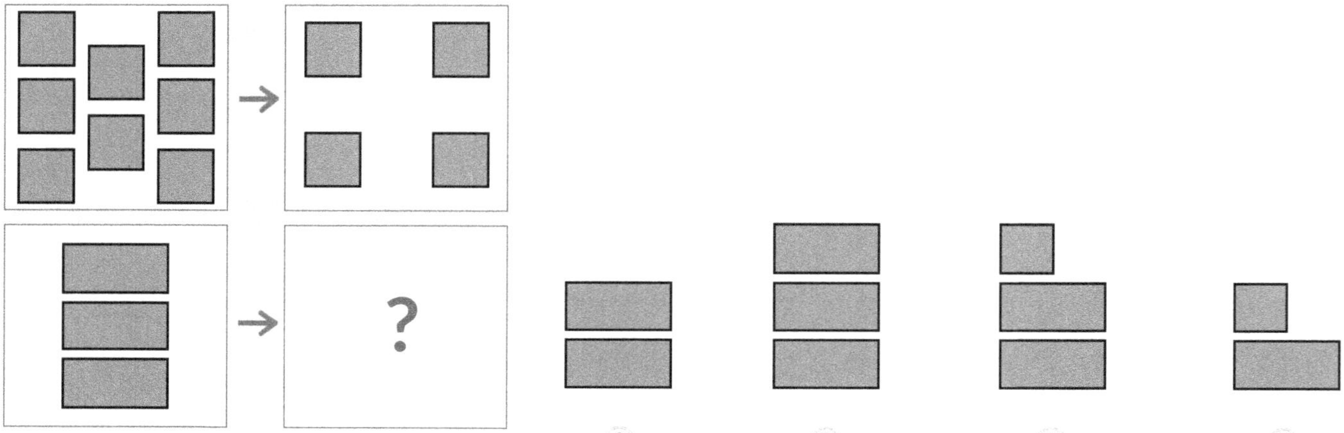

9.

10.

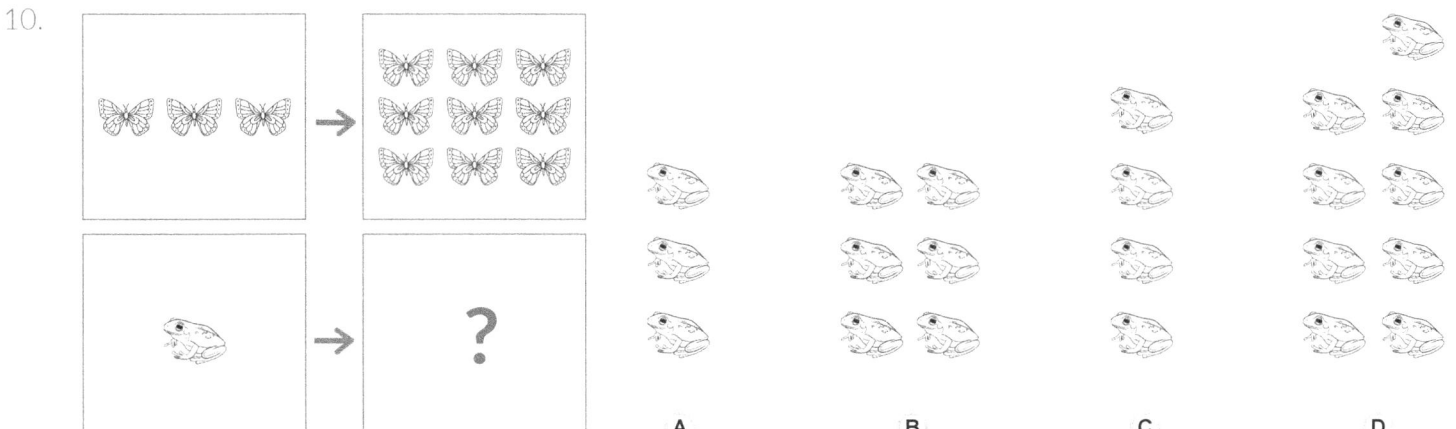

A   B   C   D

11.

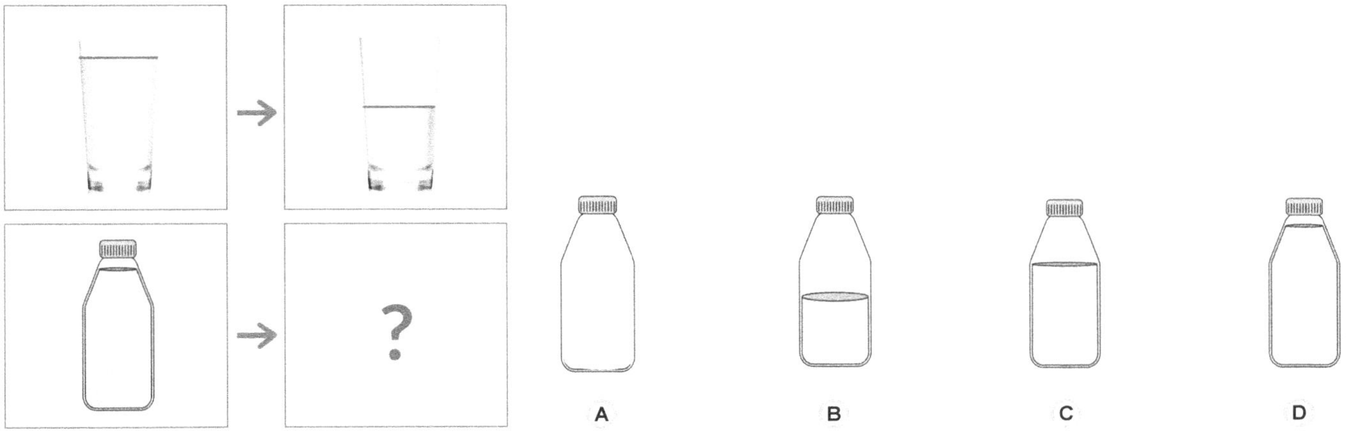

A   B   C   D

12.

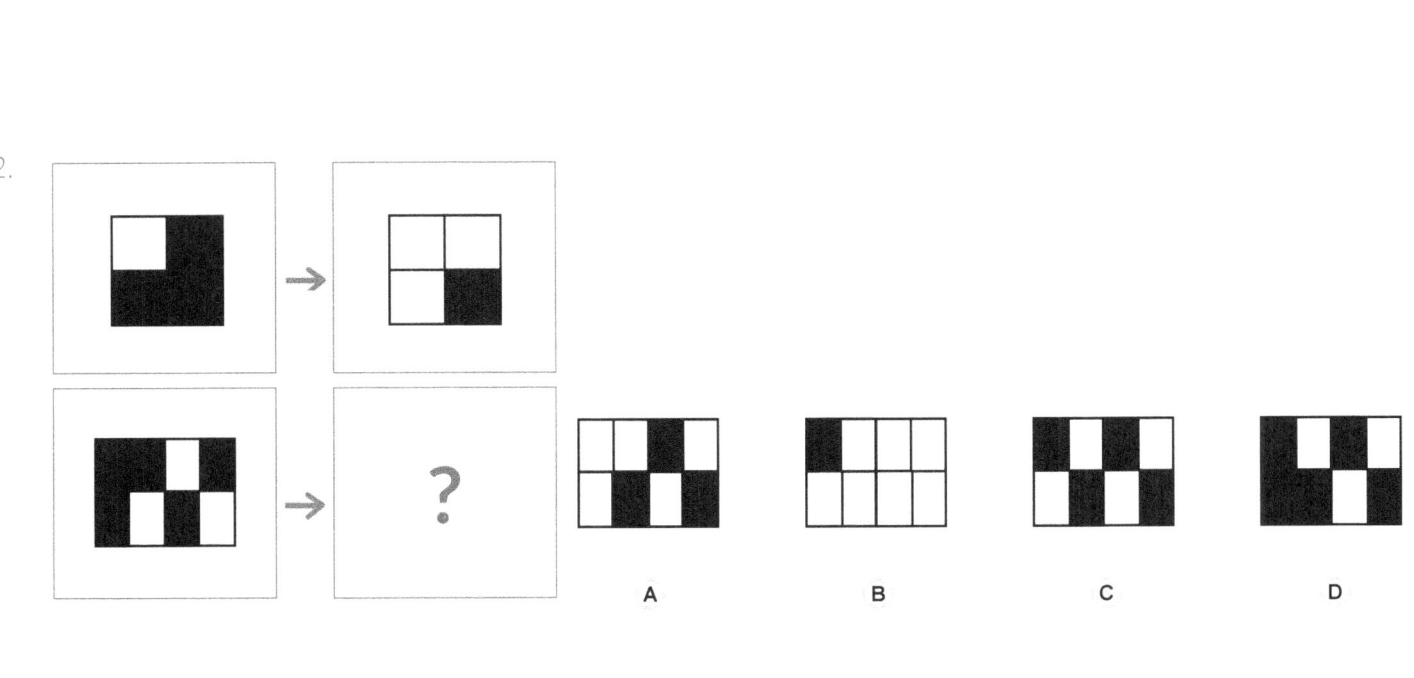

A   B   C   D

13.

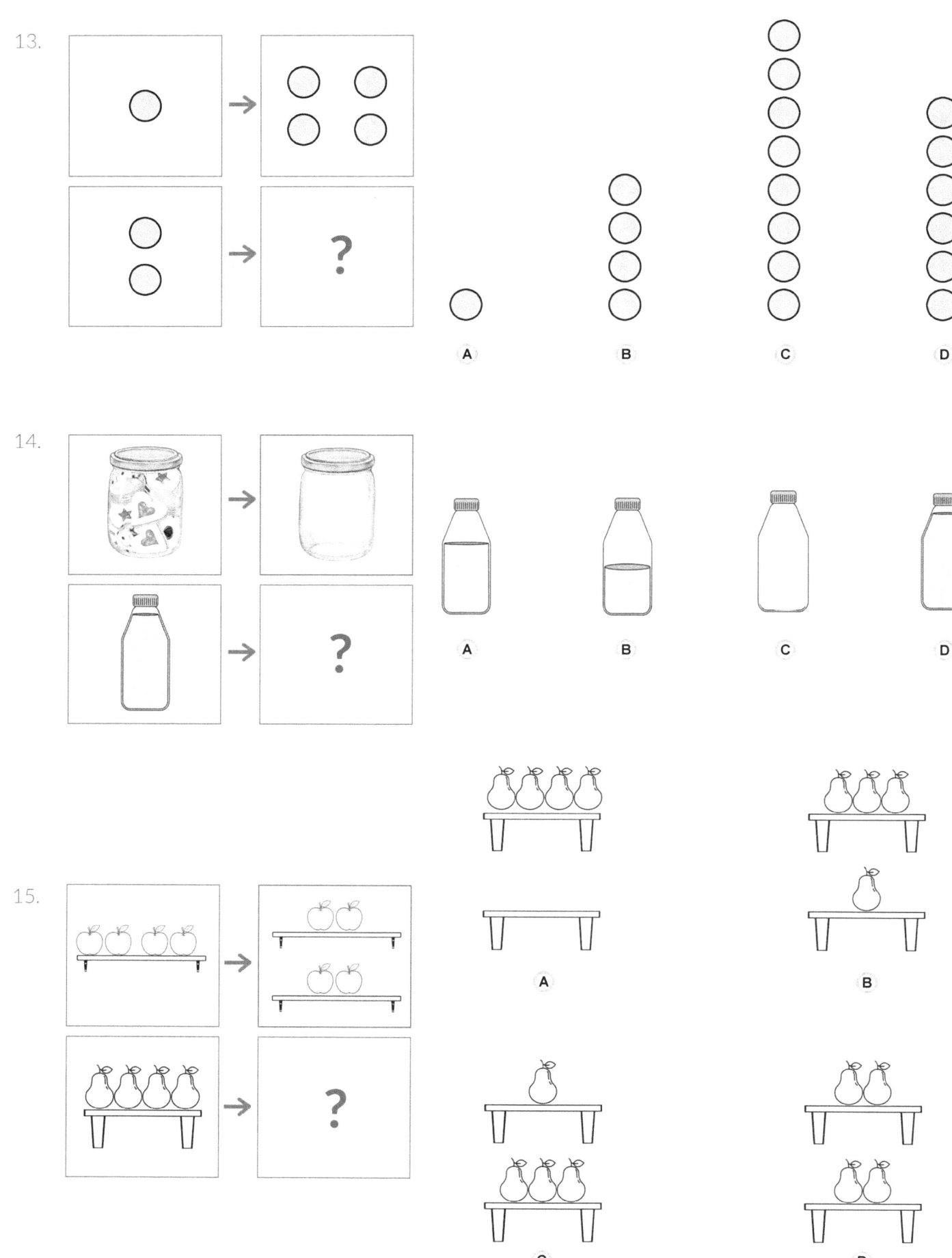

14.

15.

16.

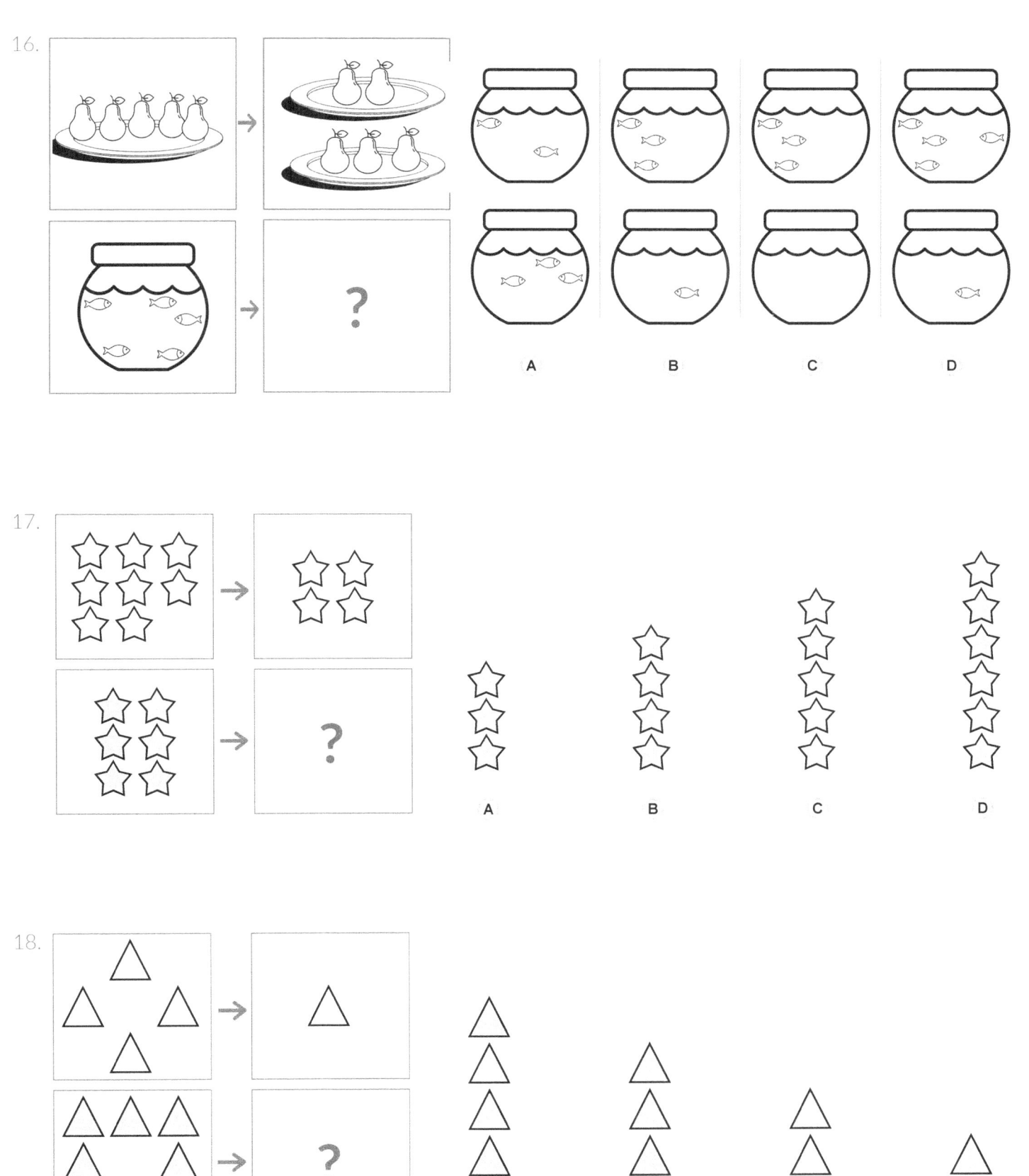

17.

18.

NUMBER PUZZLES

Which number would go in place of the box with the question mark so that both of the sides of the equal sign have the same amount?

1.

4 = 12 + 3 - $?$ 12 (A)   11 (B)   10 (C)   9 (D)

2.

8 = 11 + 9 - $?$ 12 (A)   13 (B)   14 (C)   15 (D)

3.

0 = 10 - 9 - $?$ 3 (A)   2 (B)   1 (C)   0 (D)

4.

12 = 4 - 2 + $?$ 10 (A)   11 (B)   12 (C)   0 (D)

5.

12 = 2 - 0 + $?$ 8 (A)   9 (B)   10 (C)   11 (D)

6.

3 = 11 + 2 - $?$ 8 (A)   9 (B)   10 (C)   11 (D)

7. $16 = 14 - 9 + \boxed{?}$

5	12	10	11
A	B	C	D

8. $4 = 15 - 9 - \boxed{?}$

1	2	3	4
A	B	C	D

9. $2 = 19 - 6 - \boxed{?}$

11	13	10	9
A	B	C	D

10. $14 = 17 - 8 + \boxed{?}$

15	9	5	0
A	B	C	D

11. $18 = 14 - 9 + \boxed{?}$

5	13	12	11
A	B	C	D

12. $15 = 14 - 8 + \boxed{?}$

6	7	8	9
A	B	C	D

37

13.
$$2 = 19 - 8 - \boxed{?}$$

9 (A)　　11 (B)　　5 (C)　　7 (D)

14.
$$1 = 10 + 2 - \boxed{?}$$

9 (A)　　10 (B)　　11 (C)　　8 (D)

15.
$$4 = 17 + 2 - \boxed{?}$$

15 (A)　　19 (B)　　5 (C)　　16 (D)

16.
$$5 = 15 - 10 - \boxed{?}$$

5 (A)　　0 (B)　　10 (C)　　1 (D)

17.
$$14 = 17 - 6 + \boxed{?}$$

2 (A)　　11 (B)　　8 (C)　　3 (D)

18.
$$17 = 12 - 9 + \boxed{?}$$

3 (A)　　14 (B)　　13 (C)　　15 (D)

NUMBER SERIES

Directions: Which rod goes in the place of the missing rod to finish the pattern?

1.

A   B   C   D

2.

A   B   C   D

3.

A   B   C   D

4.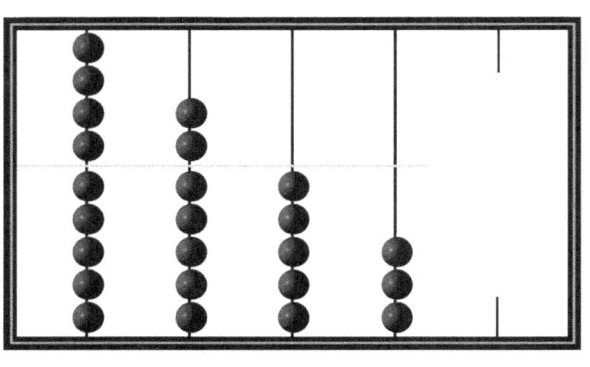

A   B   C   D

5.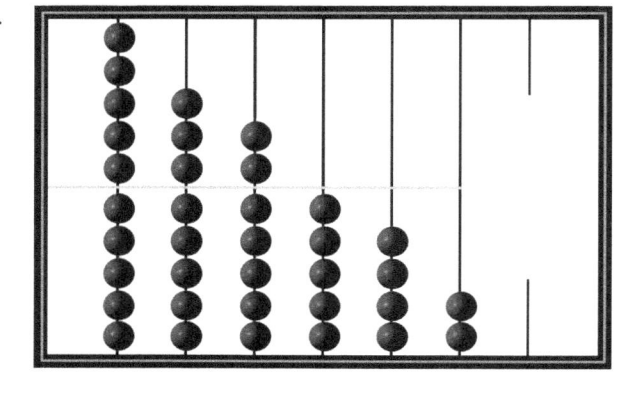

A   B   C   D

6.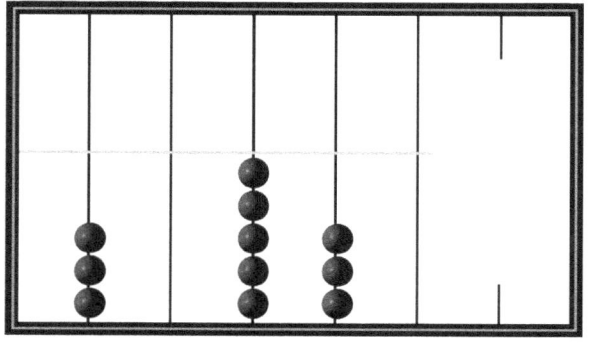

A   B   C   D

7.

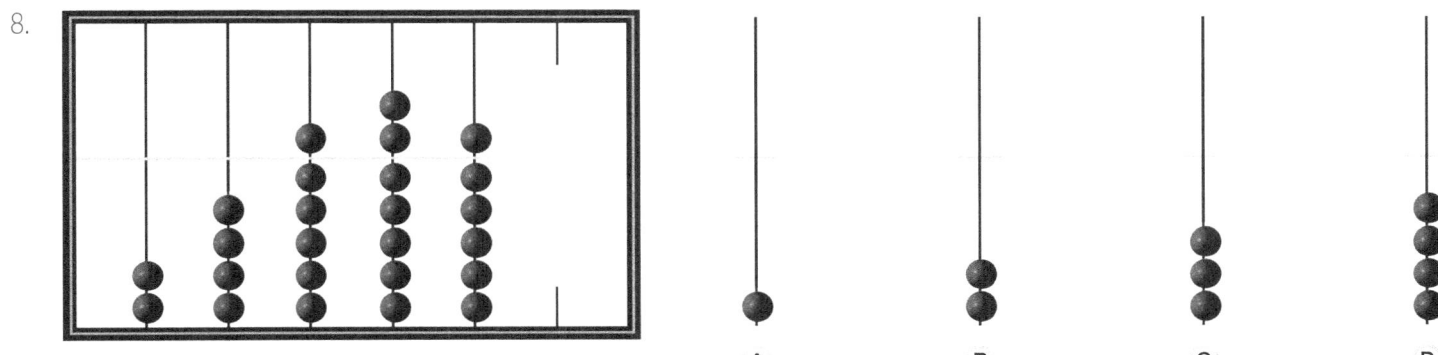

A   B   C   D

8.

A   B   C   D

9.

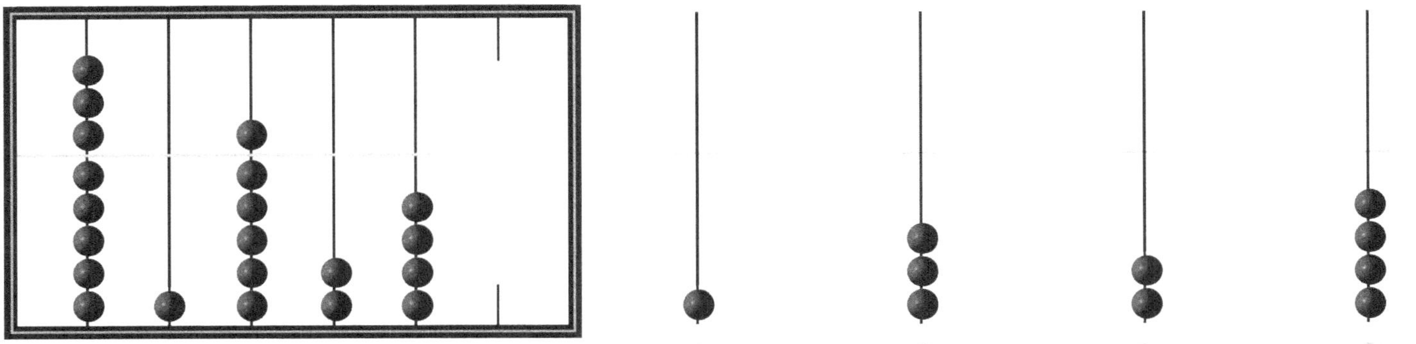

A   B   C   D

10.

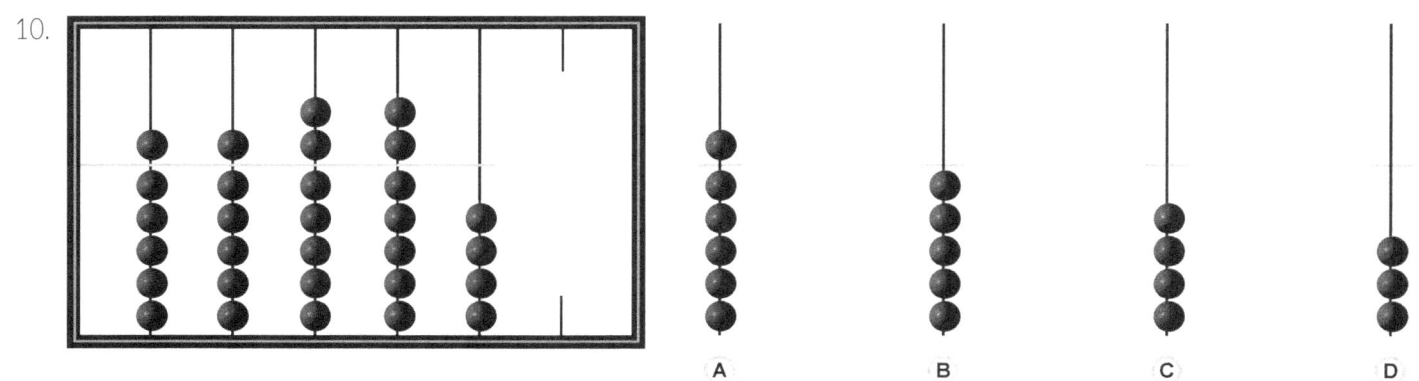

A B C D

11.

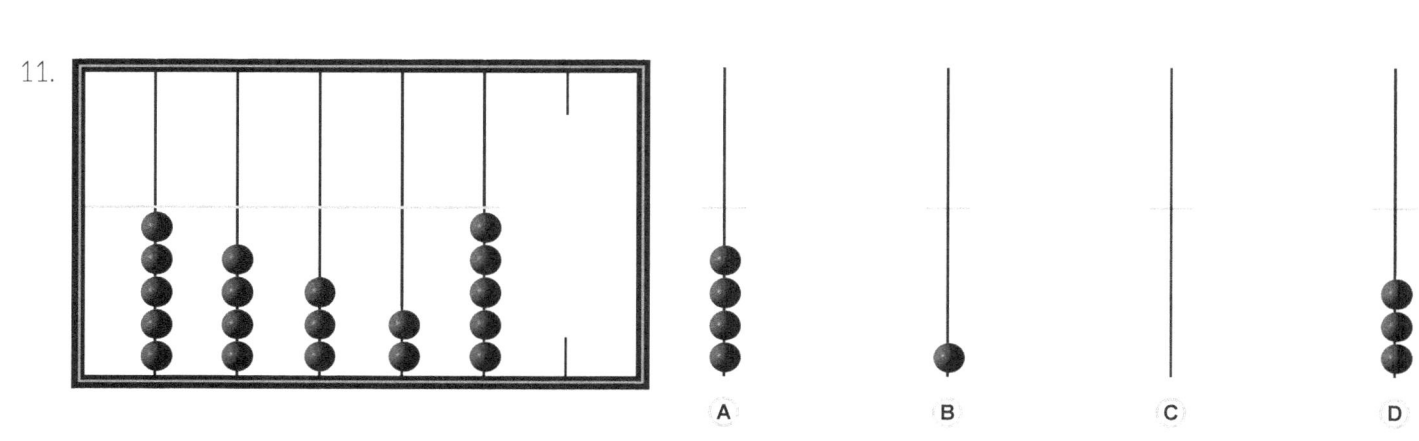

A B C D

12.

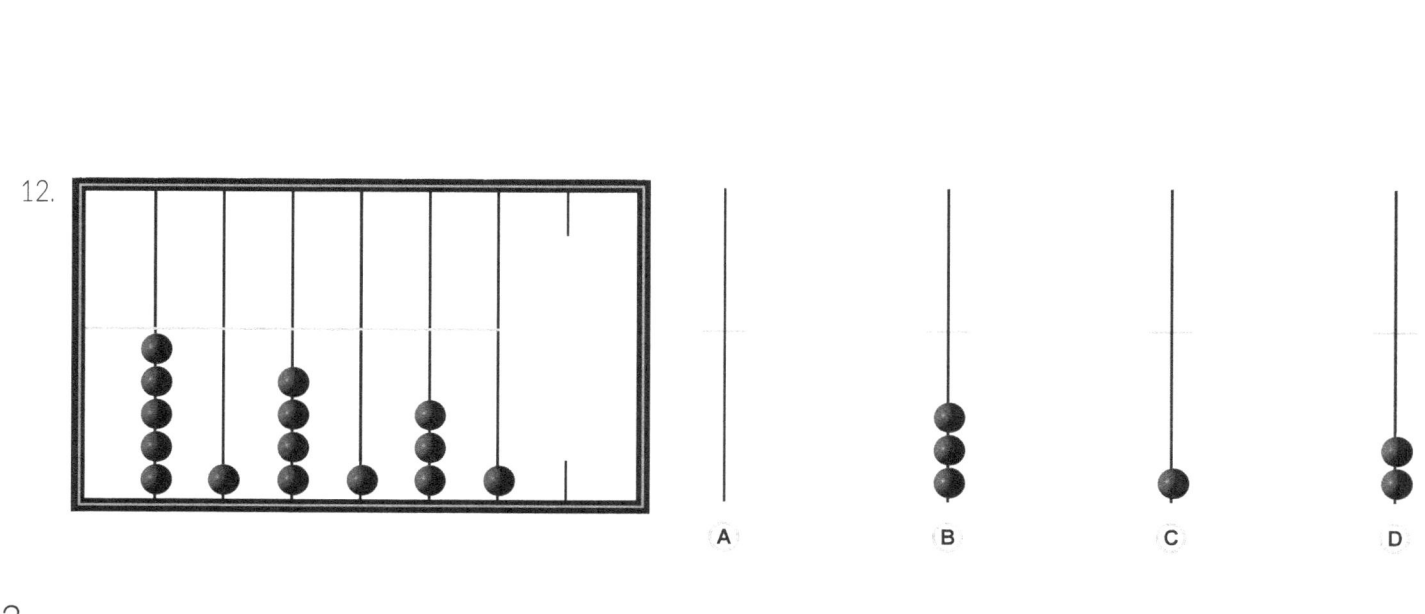

A B C D

13.

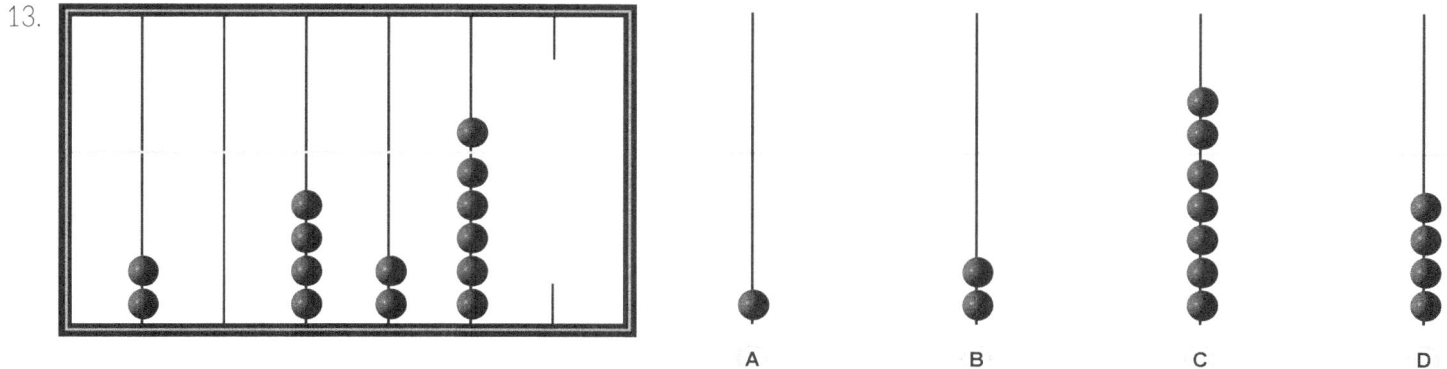

A B C D

14.

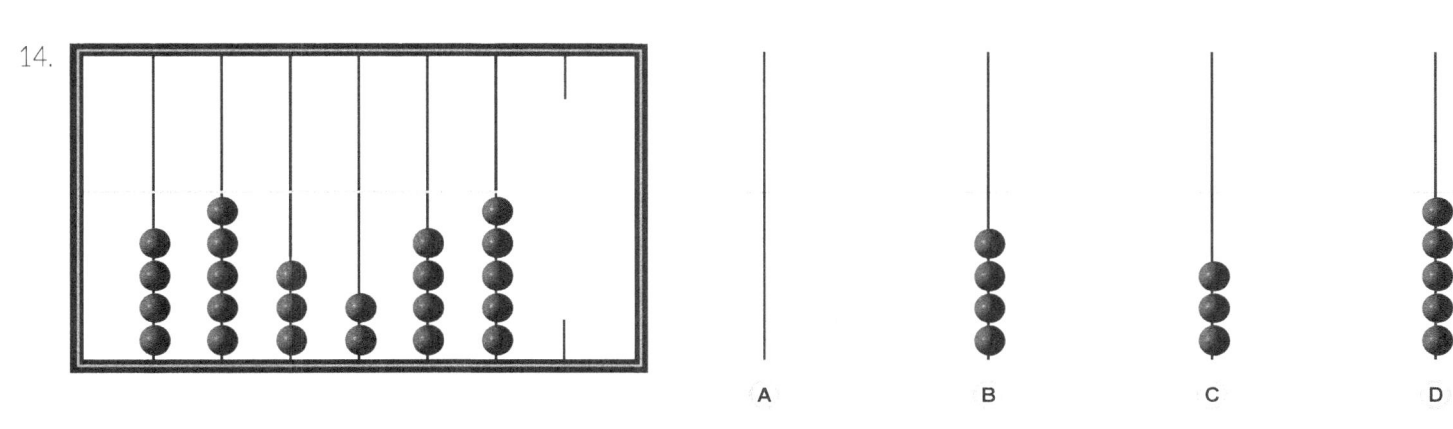

A B C D

15.

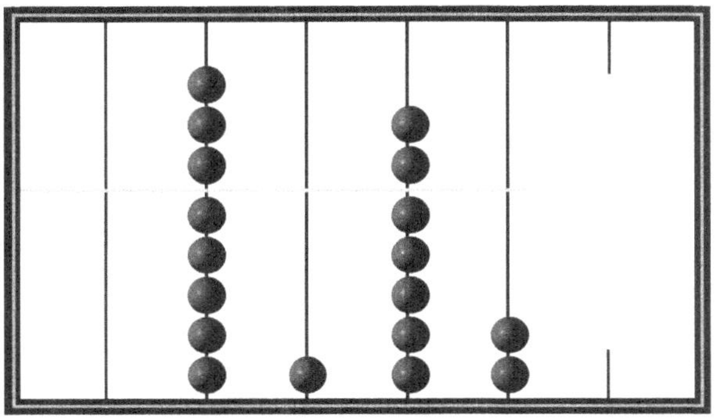

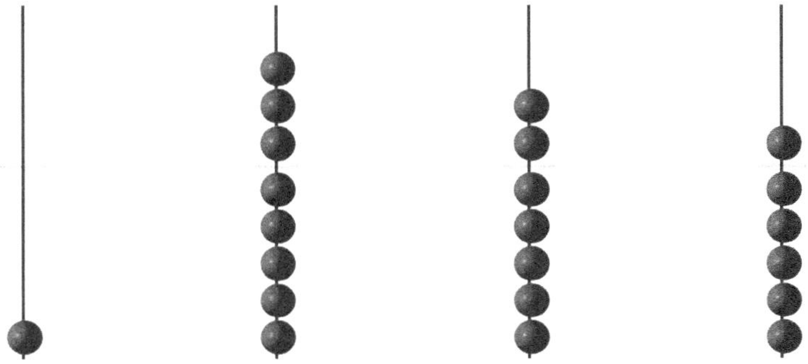

A B C D

16.

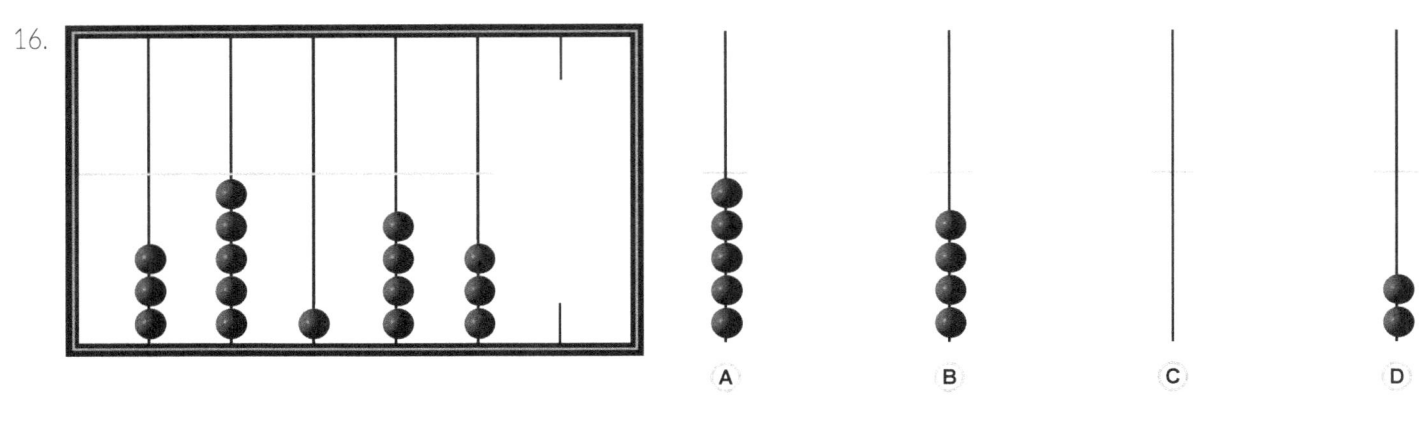

17.

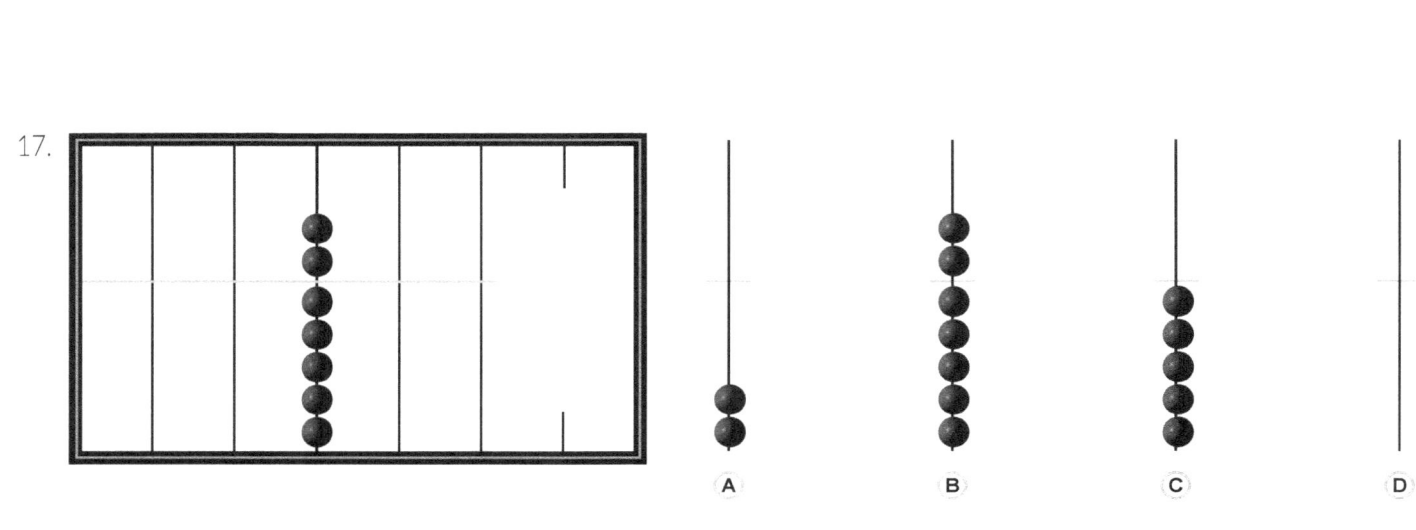

18.

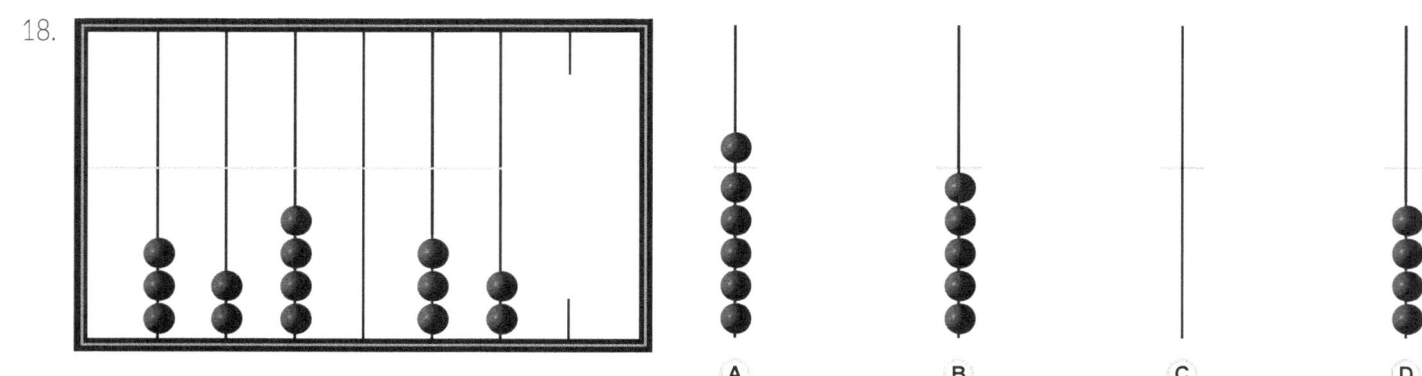

COGAT® PRACTICE TEST 3

Which answer choice goes with the picture in the bottom box in the same way the top pictures do?

1.

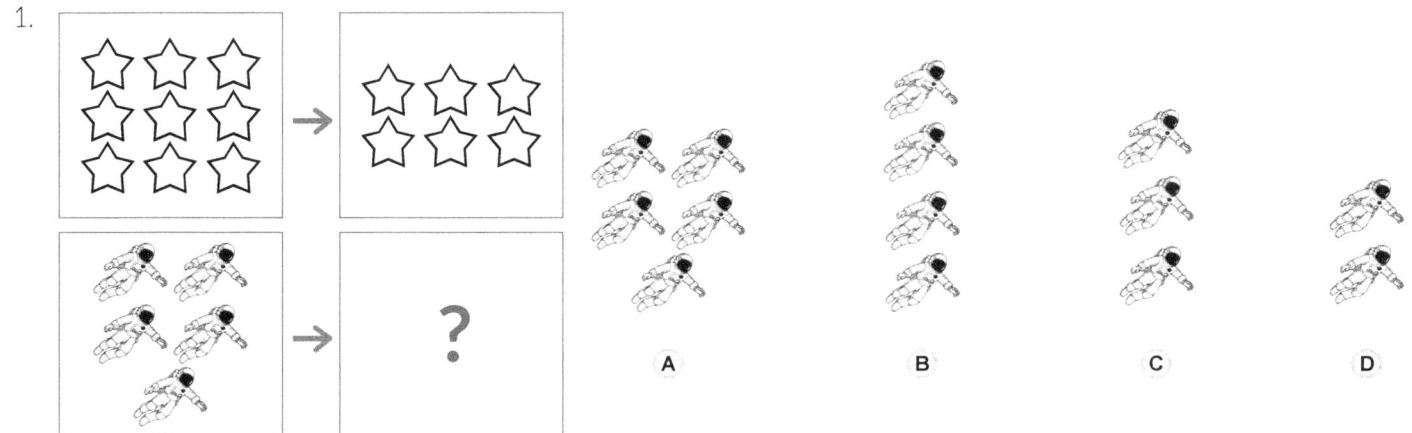

2.

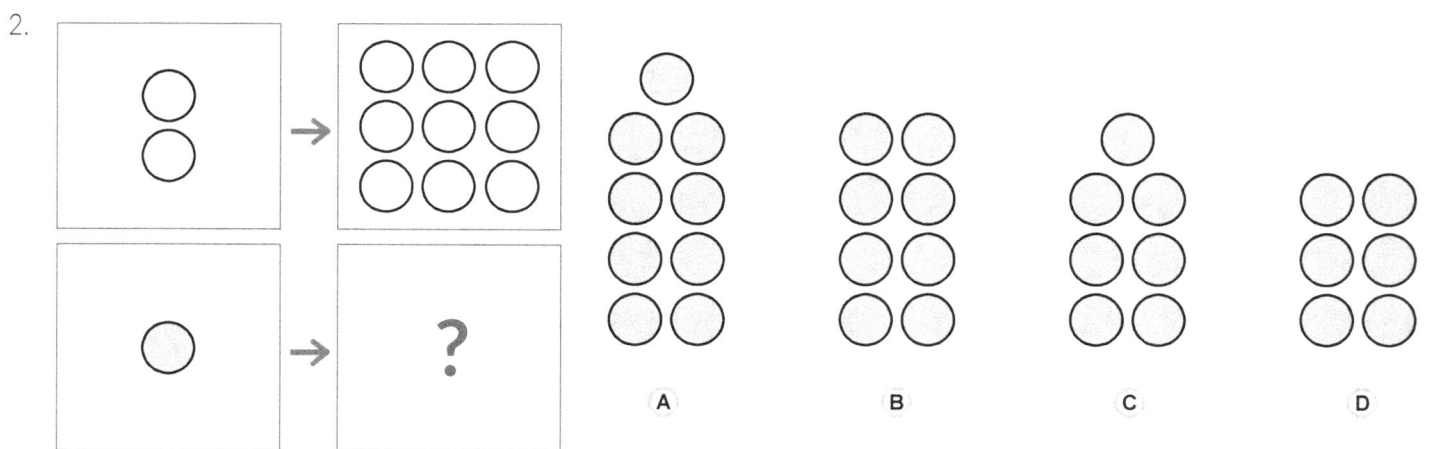

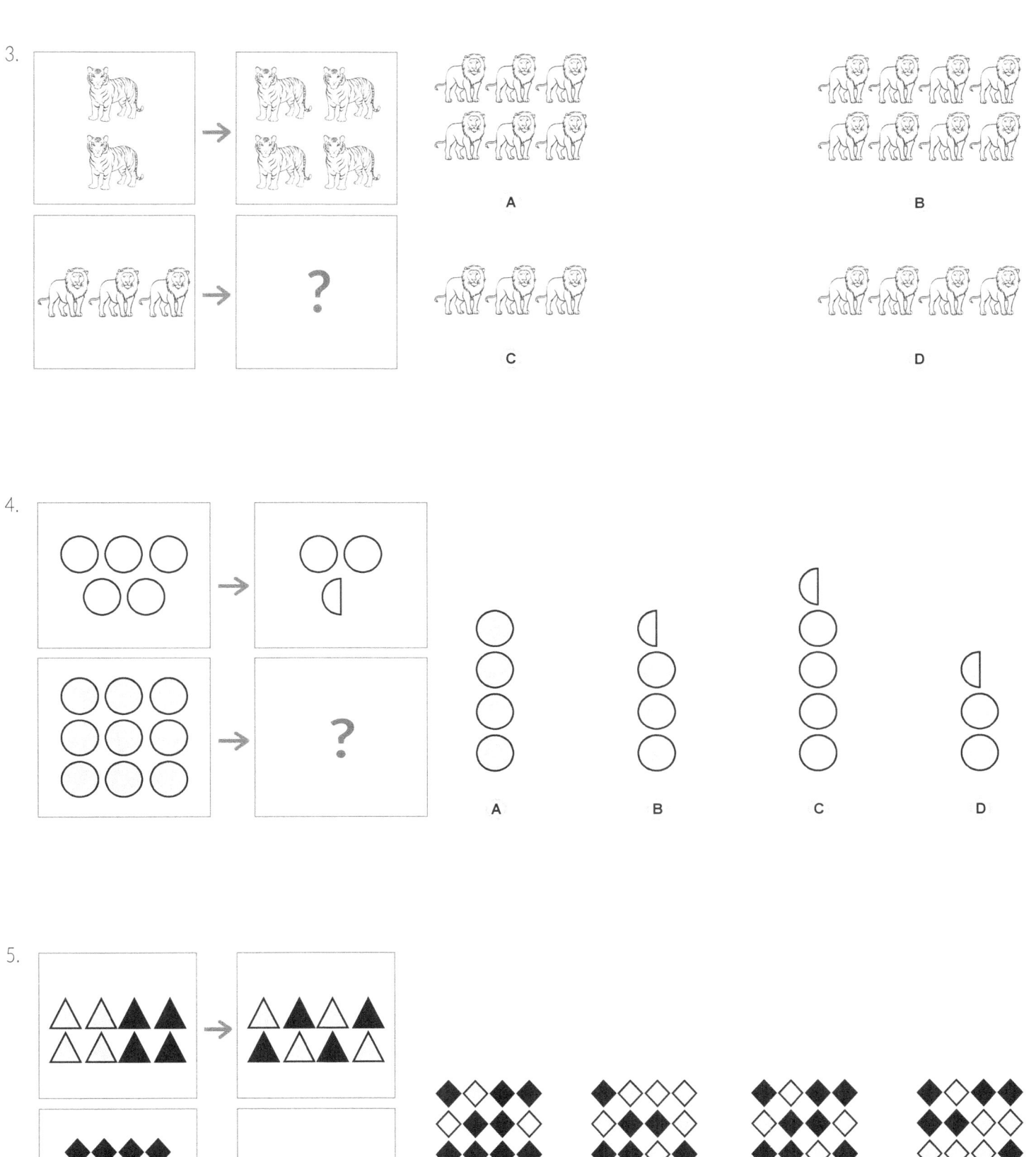

3.

A

B

C

D

4.

A B C D

5.

A B C D

47

6.

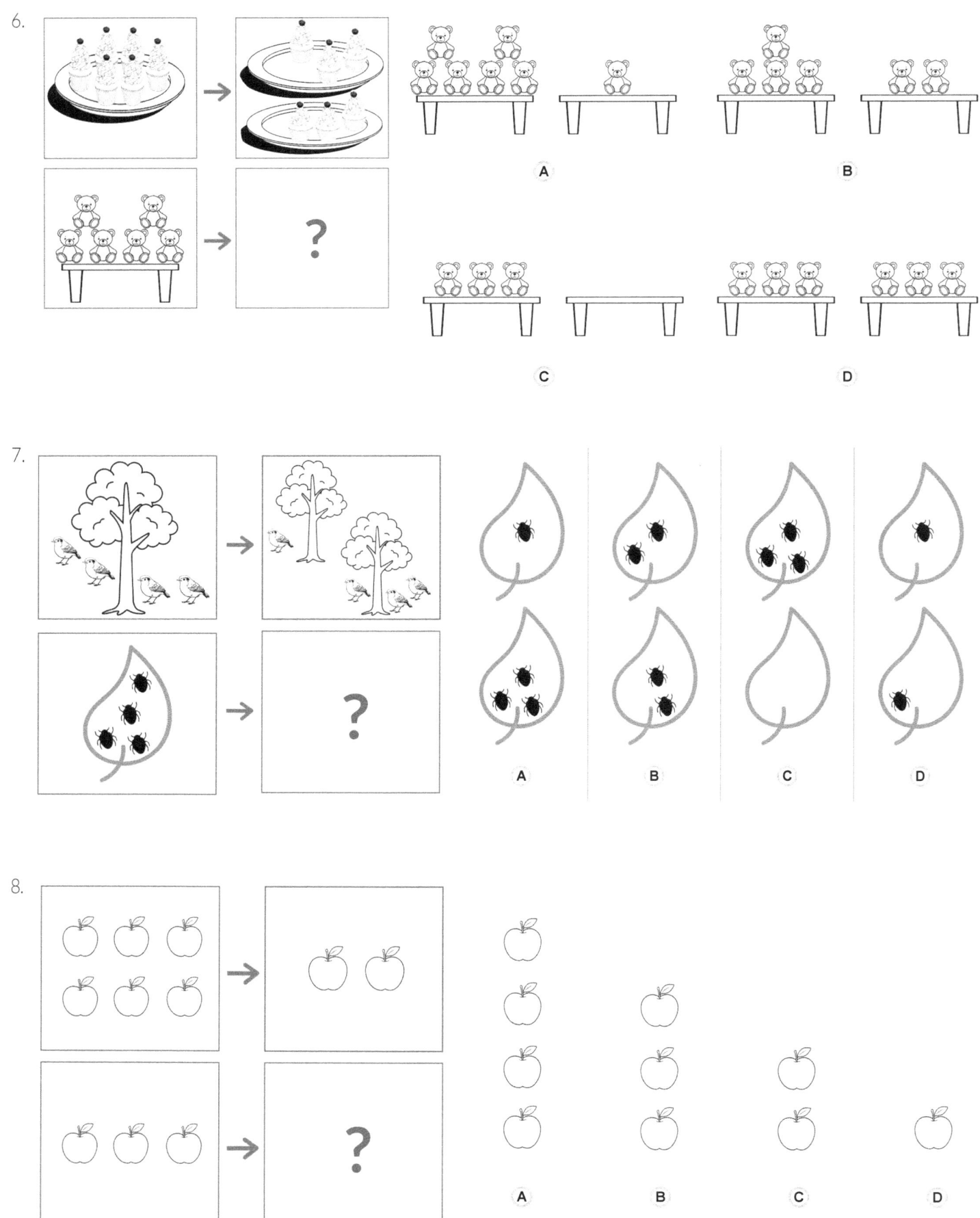

7.

8.

48

9.

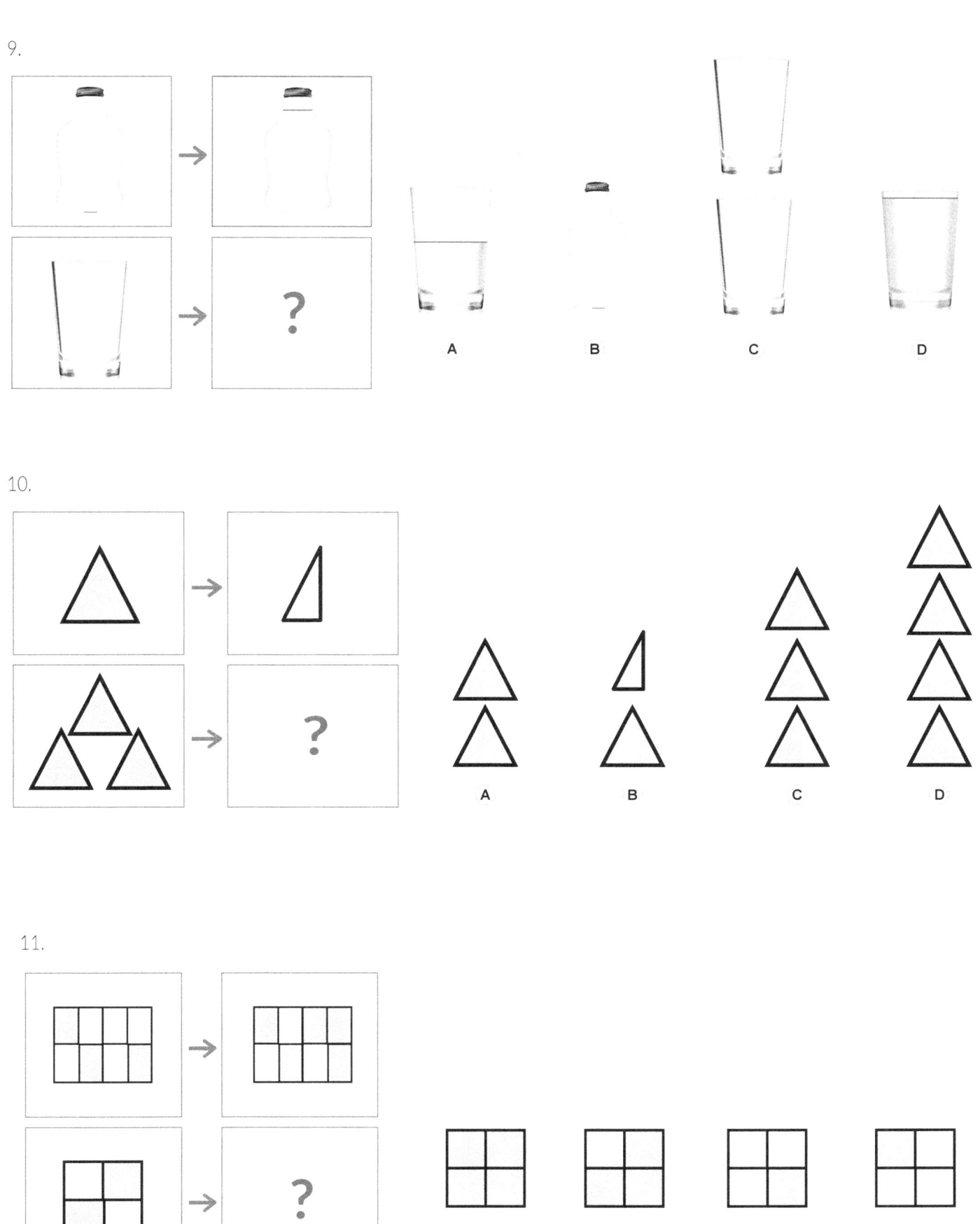

10.

11.

12.

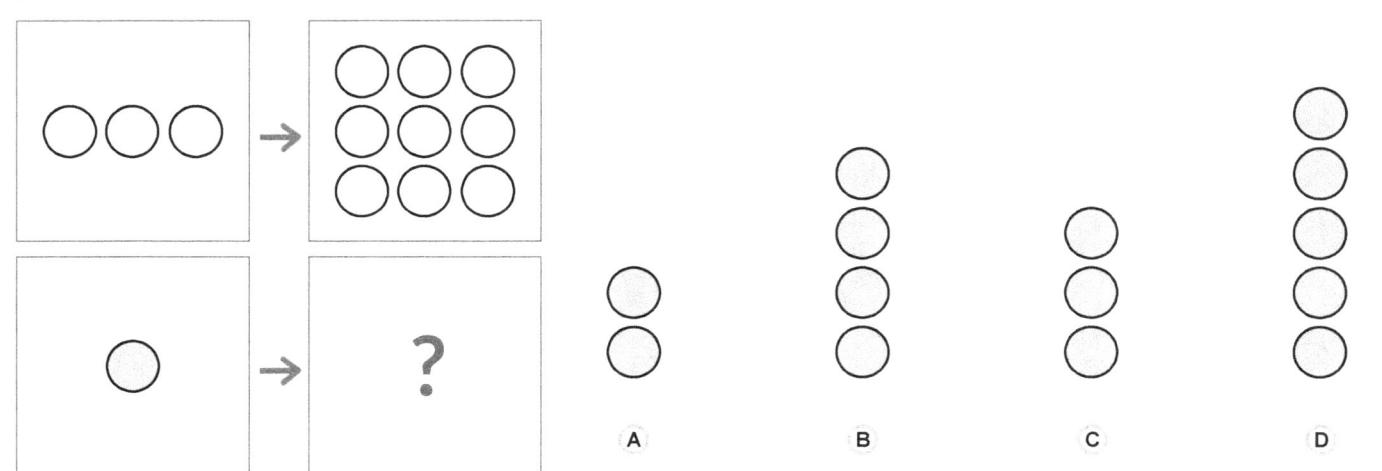

13.

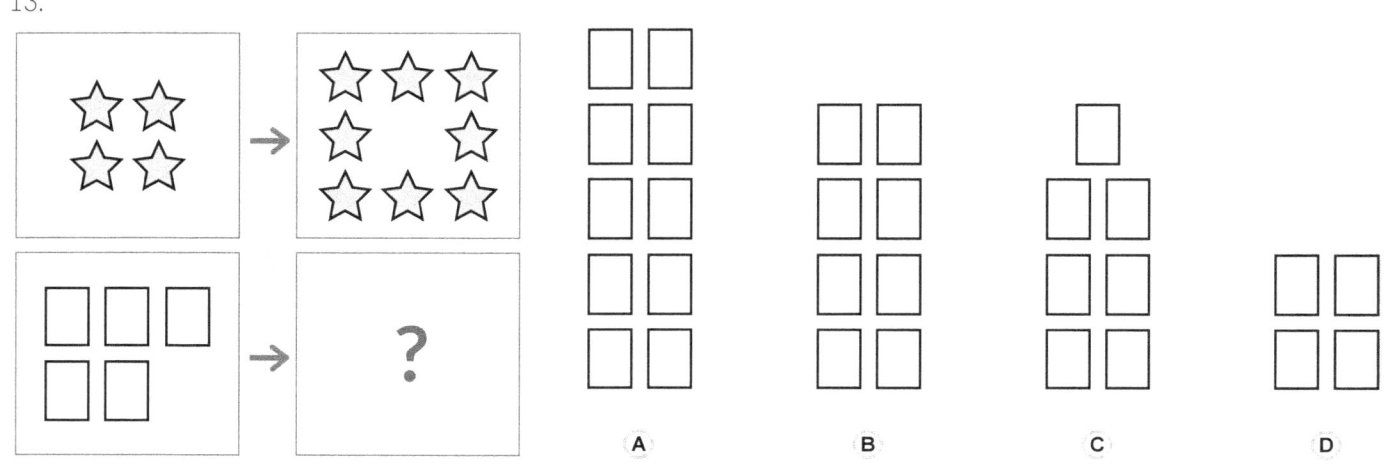

14.

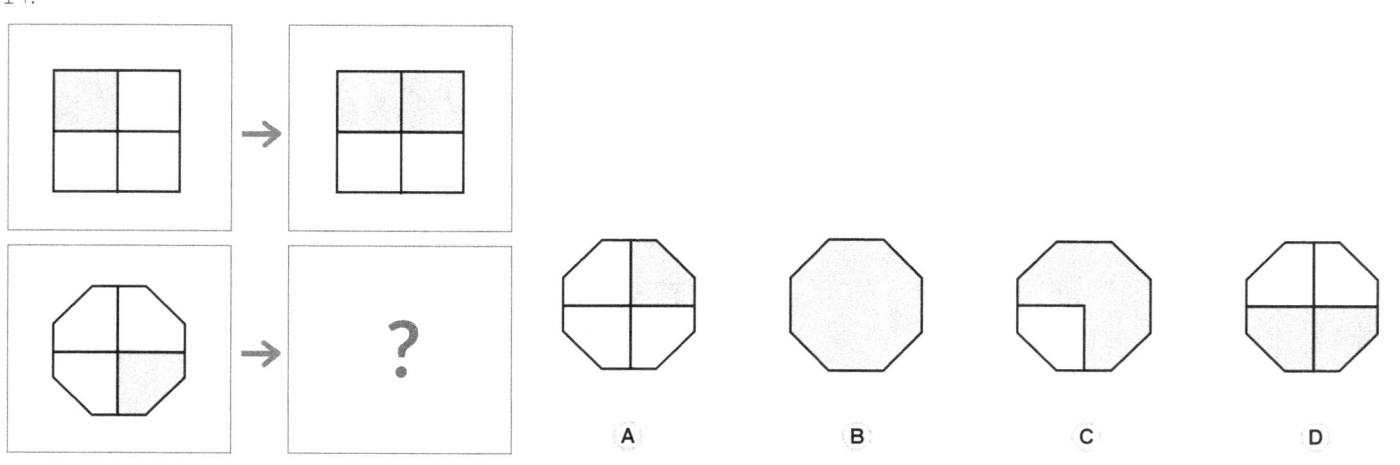

NUMBER PUZZLES

Which number would go in place of the box with the question mark so that both of the sides of the equal sign have the same amount?

1.
3 = 19 - 10 - $?$

1	9	6	7
A	B	C	D

2.
2 = 12 - 9 - $?$

0	1	3	5
A	B	C	D

3.
8 = 12 - 4 - $?$

1	8	0	4
A	B	C	D

4.
5 = 10 - 5 - $?$

5	7	1	0
A	B	C	D

5.
2 = 18 - 7 - $?$

9	2	0	4
A	B	C	D

6.
12 = 4 + 3 + $?$

7	5	3	12
A	B	C	D

51

7. $8 = 15 + 4 - \boxed{?}$
10 (A) 8 (B) 9 (C) 11 (D)

8. $3 = 19 - 4 - \boxed{?}$
1 (A) 9 (B) 12 (C) 11 (D)

9. $9 = 18 - 7 - \boxed{?}$
2 (A) 3 (B) 11 (C) 0 (D)

10. $2 = 15 - 4 - \boxed{?}$
8 (A) 9 (B) 2 (C) 11 (D)

11. $12 = 1 + 2 + \boxed{?}$
6 (A) 7 (B) 8 (C) 9 (D)

12. $1 = 17 - 8 - \boxed{?}$
8 (A) 9 (B) 7 (C) 11 (D)

13.

$$9 = 12 - 11 + \boxed{?}$$

7	8	9	0
A	B	C	D

14.

$$3 = 18 - 4 - \boxed{?}$$

14	2	11	4
A	B	C	D

15.

$$8 = 14 - 8 + \boxed{?}$$

1	2	4	6
A	B	C	D

16.

$$3 = 19 - 10 - \boxed{?}$$

0	2	6	8
A	B	C	D

CHALLENGE QUESTIONS

1.

$$2 = 1 \times \boxed{?}$$

0	1	2	3
A	B	C	D

2.

$$3 = 1 \times \boxed{?}$$

0	1	2	3
A	B	C	D

3.

$6 = 3 \times \boxed{?}$

0   1   2   3
A   B   C   D

4.

$8 = 4 \times \boxed{?}$

0   1   2   3
A   B   C   D

5.

$0 = 3 \times \boxed{?}$

0   1   2   3
A   B   C   D

6.

$10 = 5 \times \boxed{?}$

0   1   2   3
A   B   C   D

NUMBER SERIES

Directions: Which rod goes in the place of the missing rod to finish the pattern?

1.
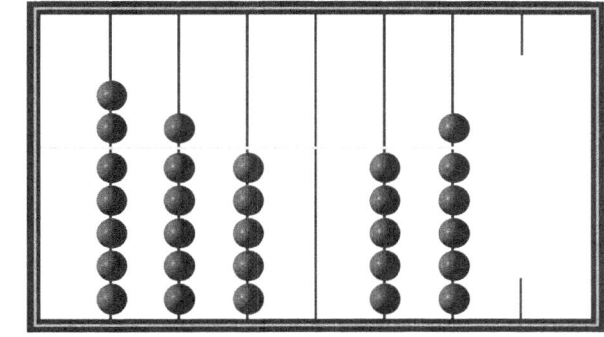

A   B   C   D

2.
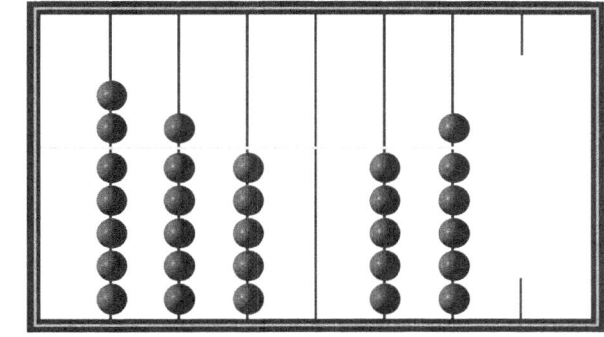

A   B   C   D

3.
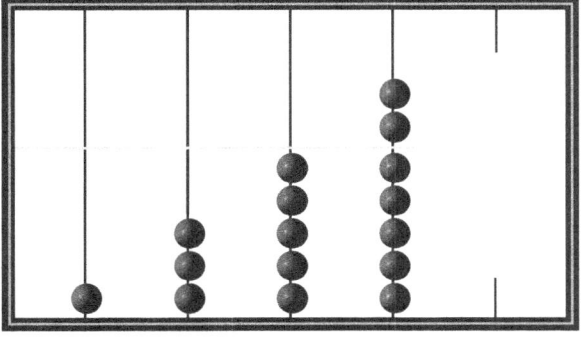

A   B   C   D

4.

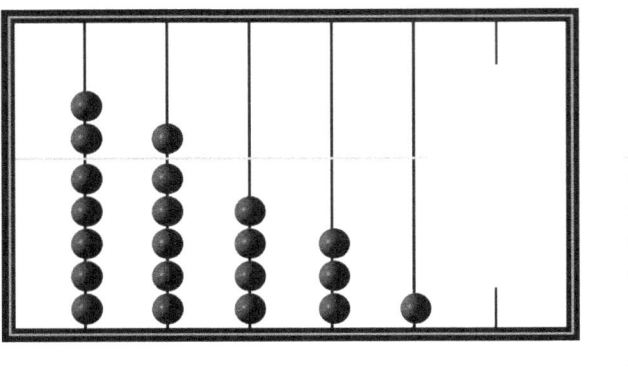

(A)   (B)   (C)   (D)

5.

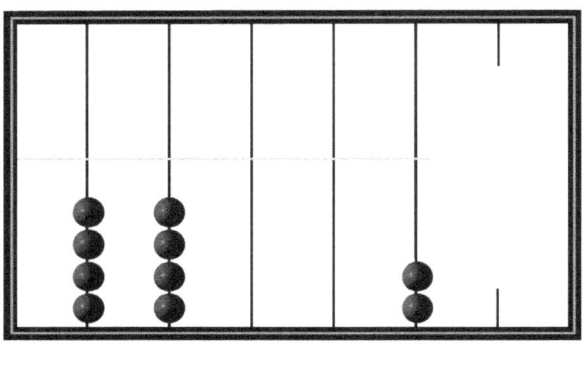

(A)   (B)   (C)   (D)

6.

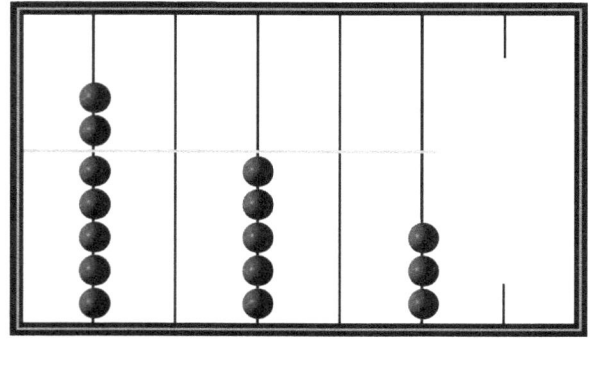

(A)   (B)   (C)   (D)

7.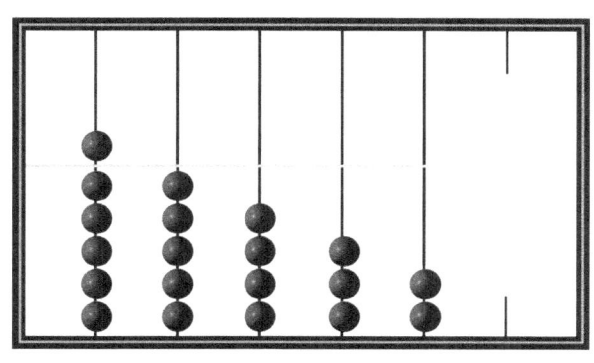

                                       A   **B**   **C**   **D**

8.

                                       A   **B**   **C**   **D**

9.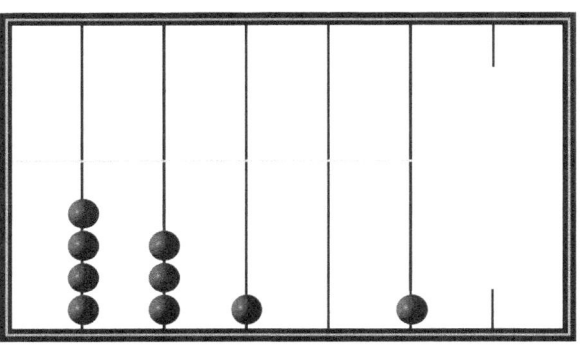

                                       A   **B**   **C**   **D**

10.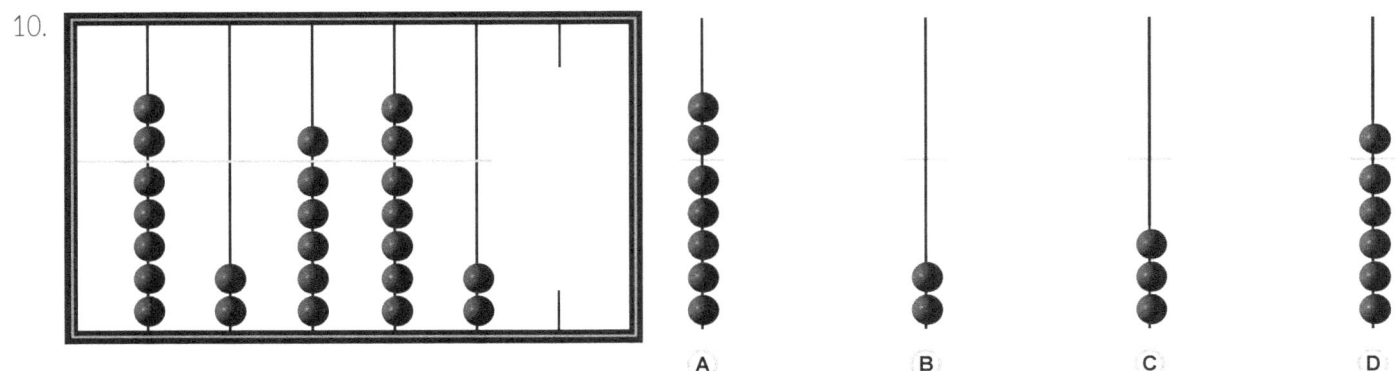

11.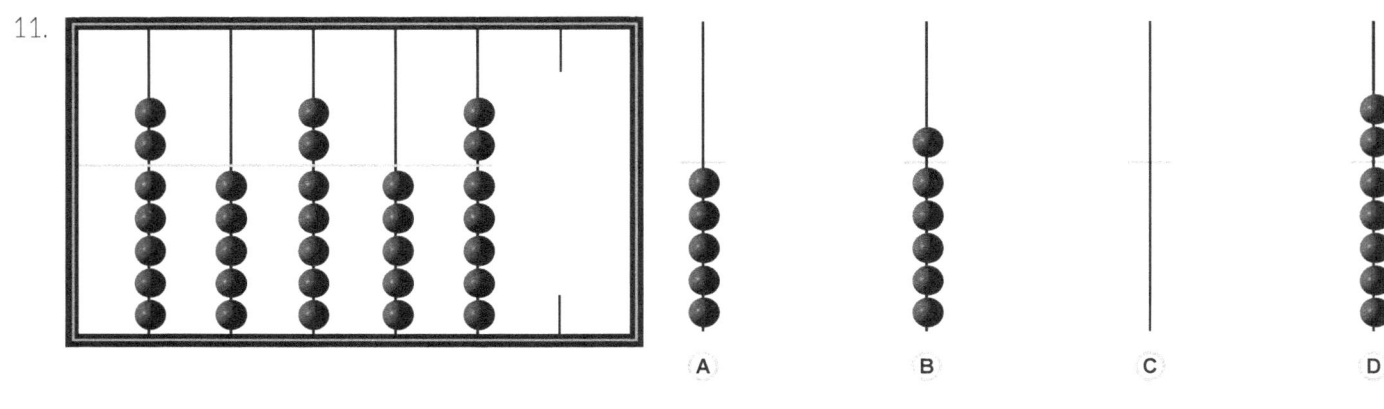

12.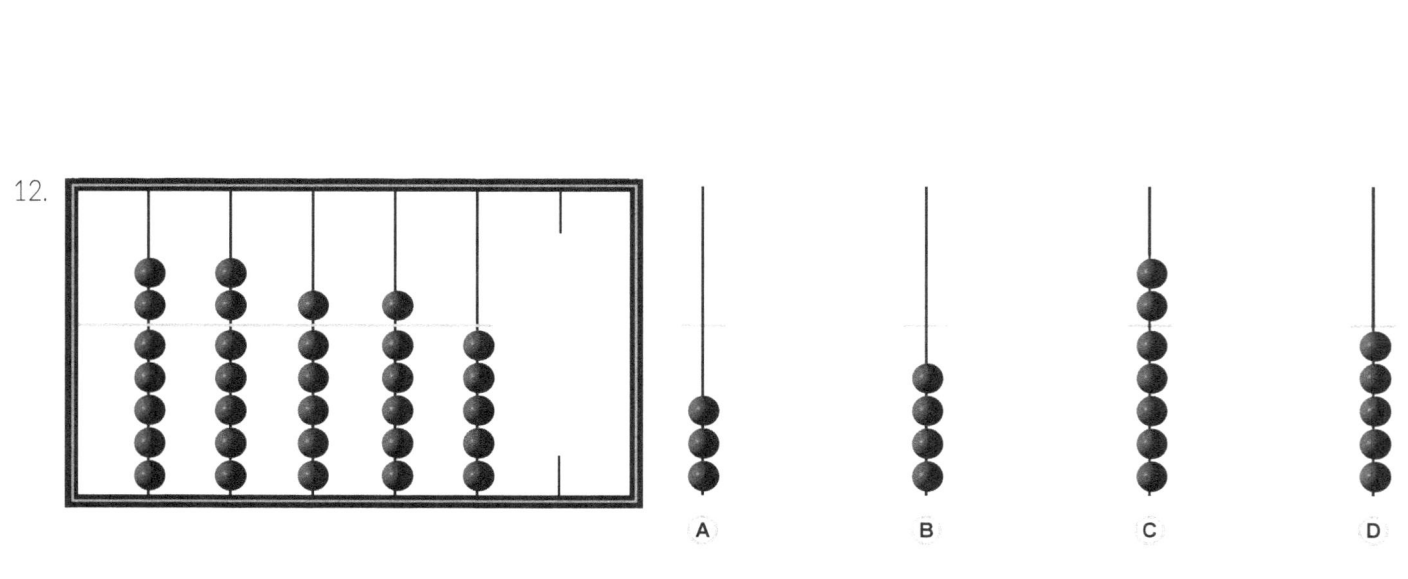

58

13.

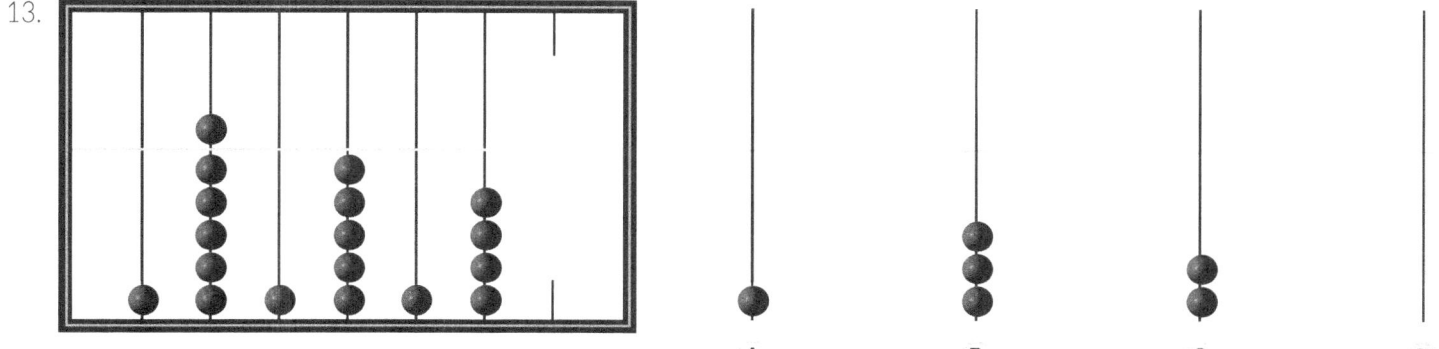

A	B	C	D

14.

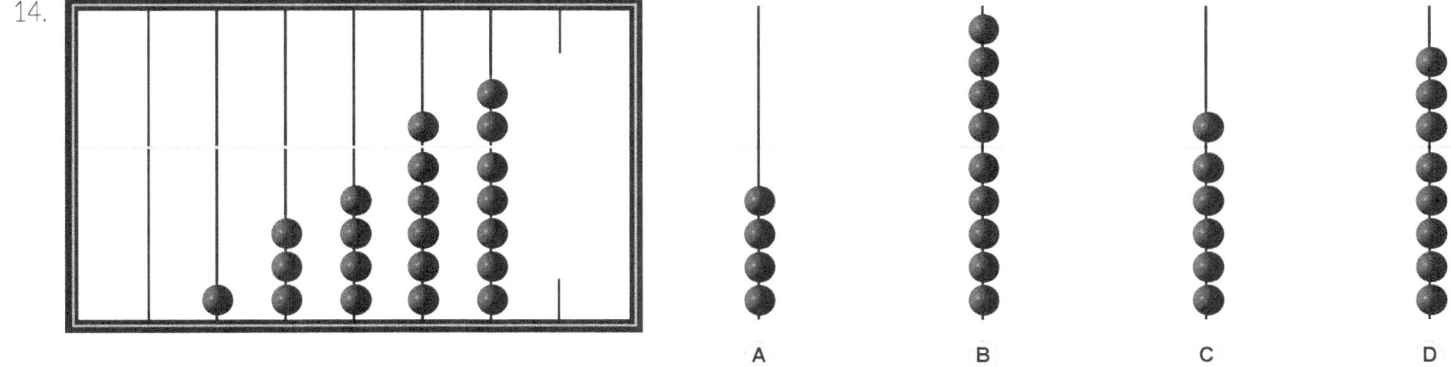

A	B	C	D

- End of Practice Test 3 -

ANSWER KEYS

ANSWER KEY FOR PRACTICE TEST 1 (WORKBOOK FORMAT)

Number Analogies, Practice Test 1

1. B. Subtract 8.

2. A. Subtract 4.

3. D. Half.

4. C. Double.

5. A. The container in the second box has more liquid than in the first box. It goes from being around half full to almost full.

6. D. On top, one of the four sections of the shape is black and the other three are white. On the bottom, half of the shape is black, and half is white.

7. C. The number of gray sections decreases by 1.

8. D. Half.

9. B. Double.

10. A. In the first box are 7 objects (apples or fish). In the second box, these 7 objects are divided into two groups: 3 objects and 4 objects.

11. A. Half.

12. D. Add 3.

13. A. Subtract 7.

14. B. Half.

15. C. Double.

16. D. Half.

17. A. Triple/multiply by 3.

18. D. Quadruple/multiply by 4.

19. A. Divide by 4.

Number Puzzles, Practice Test 1

1. B.

2. C.

3. D.

4. A.

5. B.

6. C.

7. B.

8. D.

9. A.

10. D.

11. B.

12. C.

13. A.

14. B.

15. D.

Number Series, Practice Test 1

1. A. One bead is removed each time.

2. C. Every other rod (rods in the 1st, 3rd, and 5th place) has 0 beads. Then, every other rod (rods in the 2nd, 4th, and 6th place) has 2 more beads than the previous.

3. B. Every other rod (rods in the 1st, 3rd, and 5th place) has 1 bead added. Then, every other rod (rods in the 2nd, 4th, and 6th place) has 1 bead added. Also, the difference between each set of rods is 2 beads. For example, the 1st rod has 1 bead and the 2nd rod has 3 beads.

4. A. The rods have a descending then ascending pattern: 6-5-4-0-4-5.

5. C. The pattern is: 1-6-3, 1-6-3.

6. A. Every other rod (rods in the 1st, 3rd, and 5th place) has 1 bead removed. Then, every other rod (rods in the 2nd, 4th, and 6th place) has 0 beads.

7. A. Every other rod (rods in the 1st, 3rd, and 5th place) has 1 bead removed. Then, every other rod (rods in the 2nd, 4th, and 6th place) has 1 bead added.

8. C. Every rod is repeated once: 7-7-3-3-2-2.

9. D. Every rod is repeated once: 6-6-1-1-0-0.

10. D. The rods increase and then decrease with the same pattern: 1-3-5-7-5-3.

11. B. Every other rod (rods in the 1st, 3rd, and 5th place) has 1 bead removed. Then, every other rod (rods in the 2nd, 4th, and 6th place) has 1 bead removed.

12. A. Every other rod (rods in the 1st, 3rd, and 5th place) has 1 bead added. Then, every other rod (rods in the 2nd, 4th, and 6th place) has 1 bead removed.

13. C. The rods increase and then decrease with the same pattern: 6-5-4-3-4-5.

14. B. Every other rod (rods in the 1st, 3rd, and 5th place) has 1 bead added. Then, every other rod (rods in the 2nd, 4th, and 6th place) has 6 beads.

15. A. Every other rod (rods in the 1st, 3rd, and 5th place) has 2 beads added. Then, every other rod (rods in the 2nd, 4th, and 6th place) has 2 beads added.

16. C. Every other rod (rods in the 1st, 3rd, and 5th place) has 2 beads added. Then, every other rod (rods in the 2nd, 4th, and 6th place) has 2 beads added.

17. D. Every other rod (rods in the 1st, 3rd, and 5th place) has 2 beads removed. Then, every other rod (rods in the 2nd, 4th, and 6th place) has 2 beads removed.

18. B. The pattern repeats: 2-3-1-0-2-3-1.

ANSWER KEY FOR PRACTICE TEST 2

Number Analogies, Practice Test 2

1. C. There are the same number of black/white shapes in the first box as there are in the second box.

2. A. There are the same number of objects (apples/cupcakes) in the first box as the second box.

3. D. In the first box, there are 6 objects (butterflies/bats). In the second box, these 6 objects are divided into two groups: 2 objects and 4 objects.

4. B. In the first box, the container is empty. In the second box, the container is just over half-full.

5. C. Half.

6. D. In the second box, 3 more sections become gray.

7. C. Same.

8. D. Half.

9. C. Subtract 5.

10. A. Multiply by 3.

11. B. In the first box, the container is almost full. In the second box, the container is half-full.

12. A. The first and second boxes have the opposite amount of white/black sections.

13. C. Multiply by 4.

14. C. The container goes from full to empty.

15. D. The 4 objects (apples/pears) are divided: 2 on top and 2 on bottom.

16. A. The 5 objects (pears/fish) are divided: 2 on top and 3 on bottom.

17. A. Half.

18. C. Divide by 4.

Number Puzzles, Practice Test 2

1. B.
2. A.
3. C.
4. A.
5. C.
6. C.
7. D.
8. B.
9. A.
10. C.
11. B.
12. D.
13. A.
14. C.
15. A.
16. B.
17. D.
18. B.

Number Series, Practice Test 2

1. C. Every other rod (rods in the 1st, 3rd, and 5th place) has 3 beads added. Then, every other rod (rods in the 2nd, 4th, and 6th place) has 3 beads added. Alternatively, the logic is: +1 bead, +2 beads, +1 bead, +2 beads.

2. A. The pattern is: 1-1-5-1-1-5.

3. A. The rods in the 1st, 4th, and 7th place have 0 beads: 0-1-1-0-3-3-0.

4. D. Every rod has 2 less beads.

5. B. The number of beads decreases in this pattern: subtract 2, subtract 1, subtract 2, subtract 1, etc.

6. A. The pattern repeats: 3-0-5, 3-0-5.

7. C. Each rod has 1 less bead than the previous.

8. D. The rods increase then decrease in this pattern: 2-4-6-7-6-4.

9. B. Every other rod (rods in the 1st, 3rd, and 5th place) has 2 beads removed. Then, every other rod (rods in the 2nd, 4th, and 6th place) has 1 bead added.

10. C. Every rod repeats once.

11. A. The pattern repeats: 5-4-3-2. After 5 beads will be 4 beads.

12. D. Every other rod (rods in the 1st, 3rd, and 5th place) has 1 bead removed. Then, every other rod (rods in the 2nd, 4th, and 6th place) has 1 bead.

13. D. Every other rod (rods in the 1st, 3rd, and 5th place) has 2 beads added. Then, every other rod (rods in the 2nd, 4th, and 6th place) has 2 beads added.

14. C. The pattern repeats: 4-5-3-2.

15. D. Every other rod (rods in the 1st, 3rd, and 5th place) has 1 bead added. Then, every other rod (rods in the 2nd, 4th, and 6th place) has 1 bead removed.

16. A. The pattern repeats: 3-5-1-4.

17. B. The pattern repeats: 0-0-7.

18. D. The pattern repeats: 3-2-4-0.

ANSWER KEY FOR PRACTICE TEST 3

Number Analogies, Practice Test 3

1. D. Subtract 3.

2. B. Add 7.

3. A. Double.

4. C. Half.

5. C. The second box has the same number of black/gray shapes as the first box.

6. D. The 6 objects (cupcakes/bears) are divided 3 and 3 in the second box.

7. A. The 4 objects (birds/insects) are divided 1 and 3 in the second box.

8. D. Divide by 3.

9. D. The container goes from empty to full.

10. B. Half.

11. A. The number of gray sections in the shapes increases by 2.

12. C. Multiply by 3.

13. A. Double.

14. D. The number of gray sections increases to 2.

Number Puzzles, Practice Test 3

1. C.

2. B.

3. C.

4. D.

5. A.

6. B.

Number Puzzles, Practice Test 3, continued

7. D.

8. C.

9. A.

10. B.

11. D.

12. A.

13. B.

14. C.

15. B.

16. C.

Number Puzzles, Practice Test 3, Challenge Questions

1. C.

2. D.

3. C.

4. C.

5. A.

6. C.

Number Series, Practice Test 3

1. D. Every other rod (rods in the 1st, 3rd, and 5th place) has 1 bead added. Then, every other rod (rods in the 2nd, 4th, and 6th place) has 1 bead added.

2. A. The beads decrease then increase: 7-6-5-0-5-6-7.

3. C. The beads increase by 2.

4. C. The number of beads decrease in this pattern: subtract 1, subtract 2, subtract 1, subtract 2, etc.

5. D. Every rod repeats once: 4-4-0-0-2-2.

6. A. Every other rod (rods in the 1st, 3rd, and 5th place) has 2 beads removed. Then, every other rod (rods in the 2nd, 4th, and 6th place) has 0.

7. D. The beads decrease by 1.

8. D. Every other rod (rods in the 1st, 3rd, and 5th place) has 1 bead added. Then, every other rod (rods in the 2nd, 4th, and 6th place) has 1 bead added.

9. B. The beads decrease then increase: 4-3-1-0-1-3.

10. D. The pattern repeats: 7-2-6, 7-2-6.

11. A. The pattern repeats: 7-5-7-5, etc.

12. D. The rods repeat once: 7-7-6-6-5-5.

13. A. Every other rod (rods in the 1st, 3rd, and 5th place) has 1 bead . Then, every other rod (rods in the 2nd, 4th, and 6th place) has 1 bead removed.

14. B. The number of beads increase in this pattern: add 1, add 2, add 1, add 2, etc.